PRAIRIE SOUL

PRAIRIE

S·O·U·L

Finding Grace
in the Earth
Beneath My Feet

Jeffrey A. Lockwood

SKINNER HOUSE BOOKS
Boston

Printed in Canada.
Cover design: Kathryn Sky-Peck.
Author photo: Spencer J. Schell.

ISBN 1-55896-471-1

Library of Congress Cataloging-in-Publication Data

Lockwood, Jeffrey Alan, 1960-
    Prairie soul : finding grace in the earth beneath my feet / Jeffrey Lockwood.
        p. cm.
    ISBN 1-55896-471-1 (alk. paper)
    1. Prairie ecology—Great Plains. 2. Prairies—Great Plains.
    3. Lockwood, Jeffrey Alan, 1960- 4. Spirituality. I. Title.
QH104.5.G73L63 2004
508.315'3'0978—dc22

                                    2004009643

07 06 05 04
10 9 8 7 6 5 4 3 2 1

The essay "Sanctuary" is adapted from portions of *Locust: The Devastating Rise and Mysterious Disappearance of the Insect that Shaped the American Frontier* and from essays in *Orion, Wild Earth,* and *High Country News.*

To the loves of my life:
the people, places, and creatures
of the Laramie Plains, the Goshen Hole,
and the Platte River Valley.

Table of Contents

To us also, through every star,
through every blade of grass, is not God made
visible if we will open our minds and our eyes?
—Thomas Carlyle

Prologue

"Wyoming ranchers are actually millionaires, if only they had the sense to sell their land." I knew that the gentleman who confided this to me, a university administrator I ran into at an art gallery opening, had traveled the highways of the state and had visited various communities. I imagined that he'd met plenty of legislators, civic leaders, and business moguls. But I doubted he'd met many ranchers.

Like grasses and grasshoppers, Wyoming ranchers are connected to the land in ways that defy rational analysis. These people would wilt if uprooted and wither if transplanted. Take Jim Hageman, one of Wyoming's ablest rancher-legislators. I've come to know Jim in the course of using his ranch for my studies of grasshoppers.

At age seventy-four, for Jim to leave his ranch would be to quit living. I've listened to him recount stories of his clan on bone-rattling rides across his ranch and over biscuits and gravy in his simple home near Fort Laramie. The Hagemans have raised six children and thirty foster children on the ranch.

Sunbaked and calloused, with crows' feet etched into leathery skin, Jim is a nurturer who understands the potentials and limits of that which he loves. He knows every sandy wash and rocky ridge that wanders across his expanse of parched prairie, where grasses tipped with needle-sharp seeds cling fiercely to the thin, desiccated soil, creating the tough look and harsh feel of a Marine Corps crew-cut. Cottonwood Draw provides the only hope for shade beneath grizzled, century-old trees. Thousands of windswept acres stretch between Hell Gap on the ranch's northern border to the lazy North Platte River on its south—a ribbon of liquid silt described by the pioneers as "too thick to drink and too thin to plow." His land is not pretty. But it is beautiful, especially at sunset when the grasses gleam like gold, the cottonwoods glimmer with emerald leaves, and the sky turns to sapphire.

Jim's land and his family are deeply entwined, just as Indian paintbrush is inextricably linked to the roots of sagebrush. His maternal grandfather came to the territory as a cowboy in 1879; the Hagemans accepted this land as their home eleven years before the nation accepted Wyoming as a state. And so, while Jim can readily grasp economic theory—a rancher-legislator spends a lot of time worrying about money—accepting a million dollars for his land is inconceivable.

In his days as a faculty member, the university administrator at the gallery opening had been a gifted political scientist. But therein lay the difficulty, for he had come to believe that reason and analysis could replace experience and wisdom. It takes years of education, reading, and scholarship to master the social theories of power and value. It takes even longer to come to know a land and its people.

Here Are My Conditions

Now I possess and am possessed of the land where I would be,
And the curve of half Earth's generous breast shall sooth and
ravish me!
—Rudyard Kipling

LANDSCAPES ARE MIRRORS of our dreams, reflecting the texture and topography of our lives. I've lived on the high plains of the Laramie Valley for seventeen years. That's about four times longer than the average American stays put, and this is the only place that my children have called home. But I've traveled perhaps more and longer than a good husband and father might, so I know other vistas.

Driving to my parents' home in Albuquerque, approaching the Sandia mountains, stirs memories of twenty-two years with my wife. Our first date was more than a quarter-century ago—sweethearts at Sandia High School, named for the mountains and providing an auspicious setting for a lifelong love to begin. On our drive back into New Mexico, the range peeks over the horizon from forty miles away. With each passing minute, the mountains grow steadily but imperceptibly until they become the single, defining feature of the world. Mountains and lovers orient our lives.

Rifts in the earth evoke the glories and tragedies of life. I remember the grueling drive across the desert in a sky-blue station wagon in 1972. We parked at the cabins set back a few hundred feet from the rim of the Grand Canyon, and I sauntered to the edge with the bored arrogance of adolescence. In a matter of no more than twenty paces, the earth opened at my feet. I felt the air being sucked from my chest and the pounding of my heart. Like the death of a loved one or the birth of a child, the depth and breadth of that abyss could only be experienced, never described. Such times of awe, humility, and reverence are beyond our imaginings.

I've lived for a few months at the edge of a forest—lovely, dark, and deep. Trees form a demure canopy over a soft bed of leaves and the air is thick with the musky scent of fertility. I know why my friend Diana insists on calling deforestation "rape." And I think I understand what George Meredith meant when he wrote, "Enter these enchanted woods, You who dare." To live in a forested land is to know a primal womb, the insistent pulse of life.

Desert was the landscape of my childhood. On the mesa behind our house in New Mexico, my brother and I hunted lizards, which we sold to the neighborhood pet store for a quarter each. A good day's hunting worked out to about eighteen cents an hour. By afternoon, the reptiles became difficult to flush from their shady refuges and we became flushed with the Southwestern sun. Heat exhaustion is an object lesson in humility. A mother waiting with a pitcher of iced tea personifies a child's need for protection from the harshness of the world. And so we played in the desert, but we didn't live in the desert. Like everyone else, we lived in a stuccoed house with a swamp cooler. Growing up in the desert was a constant reminder of our limits.

The coast is a landscape of joyful terror. I love to wade in the surf, but something changes when my feet no longer touch bottom. The seashore reminds me of a meeting I attended at the headquarters of a multinational corporation. It was fun to wear a tie and walk at the tidal edge of power and wealth for a few hours. Drawn in further, the undertow of unspoken dealmaking began to scare me. At the end of the day, they promised to call me, but to my relief the project never resurfaced. Skimming along the surface of the ocean is exhilarating, until I lose sight of land. Then a whirlpool of anxiety sucks the glassy surface of my world into the unfathomable, jade-green depths.

If you close your eyes and throw a dart at a world map, there's a seven-in-ten chance that you'll hit an ocean. But if the dart strikes land, the odds are the same that it will be hit a grassland. Oceans of water and seas of grass are the *leit motif* of our planet. And just as oceans have unique qualities and personalities, not all treeless landscapes are the same. The grasses of the North American prairie once reached to the shoulders of the bison, and the blackness of the soil crept deeper than graves of the pioneers. The tall grasses—gentle, vulnerable, mortal—rippled in the wind. Fire and drought could not rend the living fabric but plows and pavement proved lethal. After surviving four million sunrises, this sea of grass is drained of its vitality, shriveled to a pathetic remnant of its former glory. In contrast, the North American short-grass prairie, or steppe, perseveres. Its grasses are too stunted and sparse to conceal even a prairie dog, and its shallow, alkaline soils are geological newborns. But this land persists. Settlers tried to tame the sere basins that stretched between the snow-capped mountain ranges. Farmers plowed and planted the shortgrass prairie and harvested despair and dust. We might drain an inland sea, but the steppe has oceanic power that is unrelenting and unforgiving. Like seasoned sailors, a few ranchers adapted to, rather than struggled against, the land.

The shortgrass prairie is devoid of the peaks and valleys of human drama. This landscape mirrors the mundane quality of lives, belying the fantasy that our existence is cloaked in excitement. Perhaps this is why we do not cherish these harsh lands. National Parks and wilderness areas were not created to protect the emptiness of these grasslands. We don't need nature reflecting the uniformity of our slowly unfolding days.

In the midst of this landscape, awareness is stretched to the curvature of the earth. I am drawn to the infinity that lies just past the ever-receding horizon. I am a mote, a point on an immense sphere suspended in a cosmos that stretches beyond imagination. Here I am utterly lost and aware that while I am absolutely unique, so are the other six billion humans on the earth. This grassland, like the immensity of society, is not intentionally hurtful. Malevolence would require that we exist as particular beings worthy of being harmed. Rather, this landscape is indifferent. Our sense of self-importance withers here like the farmsteads.

A catwalk of interstate highways crosses the shortgrass prairie. In our cars, we focus on the horizon and move as quickly as we can, hoping to reach something that will affirm our existence. For all practical purposes, most lives and Western roads have no speed limits. We race along, anticipating what is to come, hoping to get there in time. For what? Our days, like the grassland, are something to be crossed on the way to sometime or somewhere else.

So why do I live on the prairie? Out of a sense of penance, a perverse psychic masochism? No, I stay because the landscape can be seen and lived in another way. If we focus on the patch of plants and creatures at our feet—rather than the horizon—and if we move slowly through the grassland rather than past it, then points of wonder and moments of beauty emerge. In this way, I see *Hesperotettix viridis* nestled in the luxuriously green, wickedly poisonous snakeweed that constitutes this grasshopper's only food. My next step flushes a robber fly, laden with its meal of a dwarf cicada, from the golden stem of *Stipa comata*. Each patch, like me, has a story—not high drama or excitement, but the good labor of living, competing and cooperating, sustaining self, and creating community.

And when I slow my pace of living so that I truly see the grassland, then my life comes into focus. The ordinary moments—weeding the garden with my daughter, fishing with my son, explaining a concept to a student, drinking coffee with friends—become worthy of living, infused with meaning. The grassland is a setting that reflects my life, evoking the depth and wonder of the eternal present. Every seed on the grassland, any touch of my wife, each word I write means nothing—and everything.

The grassland is not only a reflection of myself but a gateway to the ultimate manifestation of the infinite and the infinitesimal, the universal and the particular. Whatever else God might mean, to merit our reverence God must be transcendent. And to deserve our awareness, God must be immanent. When people tell me they are atheists, I always ask what sort of God it is that they don't believe in. And often, I find that I can join in their disbelief of an angry, vindictive, or cruel deity. There are a lot of Gods not worthy of our faith.

As a child, I was taught that God asked everything of me: total devotion and absolute obedience. Motivated by fear and awe, I tried for years to meet this demand. But I came to wonder what God could possibly want, let alone need, from me. To be fair, it seems that the Creation should expect more of its Creator than vice versa.

And so, at risk of stepping beyond my station in the universe, I have formulated my expectations of the divine in simple terms. God ought to be able to draw me beyond the ever-receding horizon of the prairie—and to be manifest in the earth beneath my feet.

Twisted Thoughts and Crooked Roads

At any rate, I might pursue some path,
however solitary and narrow and crooked,
in which I could walk with love and reverence.
—Henry David Thoreau

MY DRIVE TO WORK is sensuous—at least when I'm headed through Sybille Canyon. The two-lane road meanders for thirty miles along the sinuous path of Sybille Creek, which flows lazily through sagebrush flats, willow thickets, cottonwood stands, and beaver ponds. Without ever feeling a precipitous drop, the traveler descends 3,300 feet from the rarified air of the Laramie plains to the farmlands breathing life into the town of Wheatland.

Here, the summers are warm enough that it is possible to cultivate crops. But my interests lie in the grasslands that stretch from the edge of the grain and alfalfa fields to the horizon. This is premium grasshopper habitat, supporting some of the most frequent outbreaks in the western United States, and it has drawn me back every year since my first studies in 1988. As an economic entomologist employed by the University of Wyoming, I've dedicated my professional life to finding better, safer, cheaper ways of managing outbreaks of rangeland grasshoppers. Devising and testing strategies for killing other creatures on the windswept grasslands is physically tiring, intellectually challenging, and spiritually exhausting. So I relish the opportunity for a contemplative transition between the manicured campus lawns and the untamed prairie grasses. The hour's drive through the canyon sets the tone for my day.

The tight curves and sweeping bends demand that I move mindfully. It helps that the deep, lichen-splattered walls of the canyon block radio reception, a normally welcome distraction on the mind-numbingly straight interstate highways. Once at my field sites, the graceful sway of the morning's drive gives way to the logistical details of sampling protocols, specimen labeling, and data collection that organize my thoughts into tables, matrices, and transects.

On the way home, with the physical and mental demands of a day's fieldwork completed, the road once again requires my attention. At dusk, a deer or turkey can appear around any corner. Soon, the soothing undulations of the road decelerate mind and body.

Last year, the Wyoming Department of Transportation began blasting, boring, and bulldozing its way through Sybille Canyon. Their long-term goal is to carve a straight path through the landscape. I'm told that this project is intended to allow truckers to exploit the road more effectively, while allowing the rest of us to save precious time. In the short-term, I'm exchanging a peaceful, winding drive for frequent opportunities to sit in my truck and wait for a diesel-belching earthmover to regurgitate its meal of chewed rock and brush. My own calculations suggest that the delays and detours encountered this summer, as dynamited mountains of rubble were shoved out and countless tons of gravel trucked in, added up to fifteen hours of my time—all in an effort to someday save me ten minutes of driving. Assuming that the project is completed on schedule, I'll have to take 120 trips through the canyon to make up for the delays during construction. These future drives will be conducted via a linear highway at a constant speed, as opposed to the earlier road that required me to slow down to twenty miles per hour on the tight curves and allowed me to accelerate to fifty or more on the few straightaways. I will no longer sense the wanderings of the creek that mimic the dynamic pace of life, with its slow, gentle bends punctuated by deep, still pools, giving way to brief, headlong riffles.

Nature provides many different paths through the landscape—none of them straight. Dry, sinuous remains of ephemeral creeks are carved into the prairie by flash floods. Wandering highways of foraging ants wend their way from an eviscerated grasshopper back to the gravelly nest. Dusty ranch roads hoping to follow the imaginary grid lines superimposed on maps of the West end up winding between hills and around rock outcroppings. The least contorted paths on the prairie might be the narrow ruts, pounded into the sere grassland by the lumbering cattle as they commute in single file from far-flung pastures to windmill-filled water tanks. On satellite images of the rangeland, the only straight edges involve human interventions. Fence lines separate overgrazed pastures from healthy grasslands. Agricultural fields, especially the mile-long alternating strips of wheat and fallow are the most conspicuous sign of a human presence. Strips of asphalt and concrete line the landscape, with the interstate highways tunneling through verdant corridors created by the plants that flourish in the moist ditches paralleling the highways. From space, the road through Sybille Canyon is nearly invisible, but once this highway is straightened into an artificial corridor, its scar on the landscape will be unmistakable.

Our highways actualize many of the cultural biases in Western society. We praise the straight and value the upright, and we deplore the twisted, whether it be a person, a thought, or an action. Highways are the ultimate expressions of our desire to forge a controlled path through, or past, nature. A straight road promises speed, efficiency, and safety—the trinity of our secular faith. To forge a linear route through the contours of a landscape is to tame the chaos of wild canyons, deranged mountains, and unruly rivers. We prefer to blast a roadcut through solid rock rather than curve around an outcropping that dares to interrupt the line between two of our population centers. Victor Hugo described the "somber sadness of right angles" that defined the urban vistas of the United States. Indeed, we number our streets so our homes and businesses can be plotted with gridlike precision. A couple of years ago, I visited Salt Lake City, where the address—or graphical coordinates—

of my hotel was 230 West and 500 South. In my travels to Europe, I've found the streets to be rambling historical artifacts—emerging, wandering, and disappearing as need, interest, and accident dictate. For six months, I lived in Canberra, the capital of Australia. This elegantly planned city restored my faith in engineering. The designer intentionally bent the streets, from minor roads to major thoroughfares. By sustaining open spaces through which the streets swept, he created the sense that you were always headed into the bush. Between this layout and having to concentrate on staying in the left lane, I managed to spend a fair amount of time being misplaced. But I'd rather be lost in Canberra than found in Salt Lake City.

Here in Sybille Canyon, they are adding a shoulder to the new highway. The current road has a sporadic strip of loose gravel that is sometimes overgrown with grasses, depending on the season and the amount of rain. If you have to pull over, it's unlikely that you'll get all four tires off the road, which means that other drivers will need to acknowledge your existence by either slowing down to pass or stopping to help. With new, wide epaulets of concrete, we can whisk by one another without having to momentarily experience, and be disturbed by, another person's misfortune. Like the alleyways and door stoops of our cities, the shoulders of our highways harbor the less fortunate. To slow for a broken-down car, allowing the stranded driver to look into my windshield, is the roadway equivalent to making eye contact with a needy person on a city sidewalk. I've been told that stopping for people puts me at physical risk, and this is true. But never to take a moment to help, to extend even a cautious offer under prudent conditions, puts me at grave spiritual risk. A friend who is teaching in Mali tells me of a village greeting that translates as, "I see you." A simple acknowledgment that another person exists is a powerful social message in our world. I'm ashamed to have so often whisked past the shoulders of life's highway, bypassing the mentally ill, the homeless, the poor, and the aged to avoid slowing my journey.

When James Gibson—the revolutionary scholar who pioneered a new, ecological approach to cognition and perception in the 1960s—spoke of *affordances* in the natural world, he referred to those paths that allow us to move with grace and respect. A climber can force a straight path up a rock face by pounding in pitons, vanquishing the mountain. But the climber who searches for hand- and toe-holds afforded by the rock dances slowly upward and comes to know the mountain.

In *Around the World in Eighty Days*, Jules Verne's main character, Phineas Fogg, crosses the mountainous western United States by train. Although a celebrant of the industrial revolution, Verne provided remarkably cogent insights into the relationship between humans and the natural world. In crossing the Sierra Nevada, Mr. Fogg notes, "The railway turned around the sides of mountains, and did not attempt to violate nature by taking the shortest cut from one point to another," and in traversing the Rocky Mountains he observes that "the engineers, instead of violating nature, avoided its difficulties by winding around, instead of penetrating the rocks."

Today, we bully and blast our way, forcing the shortest path between points. The surveyors working on the road through Sybille Canyon use lasers to assure the unswerving linearity of the future highway. The goal seems to be one of creating a strip of concrete that, when viewed on end, disappears to a point through the marvel of parallax—an ideal that they very nearly accomplished in the stretches of highway leading up to the canyon. With our increased capacity to demolish landscapes, we have forgotten the engineering legacy of the railroads.

As I walk among the creatures that first brought me to the grasslands of Wyoming, my insect guides scatter wildly, offering their own lesson on the nature of linearity. Upon first glance, the panicked flight of grasshoppers flushed from the vegetation appears to be straight. One might even expect that natural selection should promote a linear escape route that would take them efficiently and quickly away from the source of disturbance. Hopping works for small threats, but a looming figure triggers a full-fledged flight, typically ending twenty or thirty feet away. At this distance, it is difficult to see the small deviation that occurs just prior to landing.

Immediately before settling, the grasshopper makes a quick turn, reversing the course of flight and landing so as to face the direction from which it came. This last-second curl allows the grasshopper to determine if its foe is in pursuit. So it is with my passage through life. Stimulated by hope, fear, joy, or sorrow I take flight. When it seems I have gone far enough, I turn and stop, resting for a moment to see if that which provoked this leg of my journey is still there.

Perhaps they'll at least put a rest stop in Sybille Canyon.

Baring My Soles

Blessings on thee, little man,
Barefoot boy, with cheek of tan!
—John Greenleaf Whittier

TECHNICALLY SPEAKING, man never walked on the moon. Elaborate spacesuits encased the astronauts, kept them alive, and ultimately created a barrier that separated them from the lunar surface. From their stunning photographs, we can see the lunar landscape, but we can only imagine the feel of the frigid, powdery dust and jagged stones. Maybe if we fill a cake pan with flour, sprinkle in a few broken nutshells, place this mixture in the deep freeze overnight, and then stand in it the next morning, we can get a sense of what it might be like to walk on the moon. But we don't really know because nobody has ever walked on the moon.

I would guess that almost no one in my town on the

high plains of Wyoming has walked on the prairie, technically speaking. We claim to "live on the prairie," but most of us have never made intimate contact with it—pressing our bare flesh against it. Just about everyone has had occasion to stride across the grasslands wearing boots or shoes. But we invariably keep a layer of leather, rubber, or plastic between our soles and the prairie. And for good reason. Walking barefoot amidst the prickly grasses, ragged rocks, needle-leafed thistles, and low-lying cacti seems hazardous, even foolhardy. Nudity and thorns just don't seem to be a good match. So we avoid the possibility of embedding burrs, stickers, and barbs in our vulnerable flesh.

In our culture, barefootedness is a condition generally restricted to childhood. Summers, in particular, are an invitation to bare our flesh—including our soles. Growing up in New Mexico, the challenge was excessive heat. The tackier the asphalt, the faster the dash, until the final leap across the blistering sidewalk onto the cool, green lawn brought blessed relief. However, Laramie summers are short, and even then evenings are cool, often too cool for naked arms, legs—or feet. More than once I've pulled on a sweatshirt and huddled under a blanket to watch Fourth of July fireworks.

If summer is the time for exposing flesh, then water is the place for nude feet. The barefoot summers of my childhood cycled around visits to the swimming pool at the Coronado Club, with afternoons spent lounging in the standard backyard version featuring the ever-leaking aqua blue liner. The season peaked with a family vacation to the beach. My aunt Mary, uncle Chuck, and three cousins lived in Southern California, within an hour's drive of the coast. If anything could compare to the feeling of water-soaked grass after a leap from sun-softened asphalt, it was a running dive into the Pacific after crossing the Mojave Desert in a Ford Falcon station wagon without air conditioning. At the level of the sole, perhaps the more direct sensation was the cool, wet sand at the edge of the surf after a mad sprint across the scorching beach.

My current hometown has no outdoor pools and, of course, no beaches. The Laramie River—a creek by Midwestern standards, a trickle by Eastern criteria—runs through town and offers a few sandy stretches, but it's hard to swim when the water is below your knees. There are some prairie lakes, but they lack any aesthetic attraction for the would-be beachset. The mountain lakes are gorgeous, but only a masochist would contemplate their frigid embrace. So, bare feet are generally restricted to the bluegrass of backyards or the occasional frisbee game in the park.

But what would we find if we took off our shoes and actually walked on the prairie? I've tried this seemingly ill-advised encounter, and learned a few lessons in intimacy. First, as with any sort of close encounter, it is necessary to move slowly, very slowly. While a sidewalk pace might be 200 feet per minute, a barefoot walk on the prairie is a tenth of this pace. You can move faster for a brief time, but soon you'll need to stop, balance on one foot or carefully sit down and remove a spine or thorn. And with the start-and-stop technique, you'll probably average less than the slow-and-steady pace of twenty feet per minute.

My next discovery was that barefoot prairie walking dramatically shifts your visual perspective. Under normal conditions, we seem to be largely unconscious of the immediate placement of our feet, looking two or three strides ahead for potential obstacles. When I'm crossing the grasslands to get from one site to another in the course of my work with rangeland grasshoppers, I often focus on a distant landmark, assured that my heavy, leather boots will repel whatever lurks in ambush amidst the grasses and shrubs. But bare your soles and the world collapses into the present moment. Each patch of prairie becomes a new encounter, demanding its own terms, striking up its own dialogue. A clump of needle-and-thread grass with its spear-tipped seed heads requires a very different approach than a patch of coarse-and-curly buffalo grass, which is nothing like finding a clearing of soft, red dust warmed by the sun. Naked feet transform the prairie from a homogenous expanse of anonymity into a unique series of personal encounters. Each barefoot step is an exercise in mindfulness.

To begin, you lift your foot, swing it forward toward the consciously selected patch of plants and soil, and make initial contact. This first touching is tentative, a search for unseen risks. You must choose the precise placement of your foot. The mental abstraction of the encounter gives way to the actual feel of the grass and the cautious probing for hidden spines. This is the explicitly physical act of feeling anew, discovering whether the contact yields the burning pain of pierced flesh or the sublime pleasure of a soft caress.

Next, you must commit to the encounter. Shifting your weight forward, you initiate the process of pressing your bare skin into the prairie. If a clump of grass is knee-high, then gently sweeping the stems into a bed of golden straw makes for a cushioned landing and avoids both the sharpened fragments that are created when dry grasses are broken and the burrs and stones that lie beneath the mattress of flattened stems. With short grasses, you must slowly settle your foot among the bunches, working your way into their reluctant embrace. And nothing is more delightful than finding an open patch of sunbaked soil on a crisp, autumn day. With a bit of chill in the air, the radiant heat of the bare earth suffuses your body and your being. Flowing from sole to soul, the energy of the prairie becomes actualized.

The final step of stepping requires placing your full weight onto your foot, because without this shift it is quite impossible to lift your other foot and continue the cycle. And here is the point of greatest risk and reward. With this subtle but powerful transposition, whatever sharpened stones, seeds, or stems that lie beneath your foot are pressed into bare flesh. This is the point at which you must trust that you have chosen your path well and that your initial contact was true to that which lies deeper. Sometimes, you will be hurt—the grass hides a thorn or stone. More often, you press the full weight of your being into the prairie and find a mixture of smooth stems, bristly leaves, lumpy root crowns, and dusty earth.

But the encounter is not only about the risk to your flesh. This is also the moment at which you damage the prairie. Your weight snaps stems, crushes insects, and collapses burrows. Most of the time, a mindful step does little harm, but your presence is not without consequence and meaning to the prairie. Such is the paradox that the great conservationist Aldo Leopold captured in his claim that, "Man always kills the things he loves, and so we the pioneers have killed our wilderness." Although this seems a bit extreme, to live authentically in a place, one must change it and be changed by it. A genuine relationship with the land is like a deep connection with another person—each is transformed in the presence of the other. I once had a study site that I walked to every week using the same route up a rocky hillside, and two years later I could still discern the meandering route that I'd trampled through the patches of prickly pear cactus and clumps of antelope bitterbrush. Although I made that path wearing leather boots, even bare feet break the delicate soil crust, pulverize crispy lichens, and scatter seeds.

In a course I once took on comparative religions, I learned that the Jains renounce shoes (some even go naked) to avoid harming other, living creatures as they walk. This sounded a bit extreme but plausible, given my exotic and romantic images of India. Many years later, I met a Jain who was on the engineering faculty at the University of Wyoming. He was a very soft-spoken and gentle fellow. He confirmed what I'd learned and explained that monks who practice the strictest form of Jainism may also sweep the ground in front of them as they walk to further diminish the chances of crushing insects or spiders. I'm not so sure about the protective virtues of being barefoot—an ant under a naked heel is not going to fare much better than one under a sandal. The difference would be one's awareness that the ant was underfoot. I suspect that this heightened awareness may have been part of the original motive. Doing less harm or being aware of one's harm: Either purpose seems justifiable, and the origins of practices that have developed for 2,600 years are difficult to surmise. However, Jainism is not the only spiritual practice from the East that offers lessons about walking gently.

The Buddhist teacher Thich Nhat Hahn advocates the practice of walking meditation. To many of us, this would seem oxymoronic—how can we focus inwardly if we are concentrating on navigating curbs, crossing streets, and accommodating other pedestrians? He suggests that we should walk so as to "print peace and serenity on the Earth . . . . Be aware of the contact between your feet and the Earth. Walk as if you are kissing the Earth with your feet." He does not say that you must walk barefooted, but surely a kiss loses something if you are wearing a mask. To walk barefoot across the prairie is to move mindfully, to feel fully, to be in the present moment, without eyes or mind focused on the horizon. Perhaps with practice, we can walk through our neighborhoods, our downtown streets, and our shopping malls with such awareness. But the prairie seems to be a good place to learn how to walk. For me, the slow pace of the prairie is first about avoiding harm to myself. However, the act of mindful movement also allows the creatures of the prairie—the agile grasshoppers, frantic planthoppers, clumsy ground beetles, and skittering spiders—to make way for their gigantic intruder.

Crushing an insect underfoot is a rather intimate act of violence. During our graduate school days in Louisiana, my wife and I shared our mobile home with a community of cockroaches. I'd come home in the evening to find empty yogurt containers inverted on the kitchen floor. My wife could bring herself to smash the half-inch German cockroaches, but the two-inch Americans and Smoky Browns were another matter. So if she caught one of them making a dash across the floor, she simply trapped the creature, consigned it to death row, and waited for the executioner to arrive. Stepping on these insects yielded a nauseating odor and the crunching sound that gave way to a greasy slickness, sensed through the sole of a shoe, was simply unbearable. I learned how to pin the cockroaches beneath a couple of paper towels and deliver a lethal blow to the head and thorax with just enough pressure to kill the creature without rupturing the body wall. Even this made me queasy, a visceral reaction that I managed to hide from my wife through some misguided sense of manliness.

Most invertebrates don't have voices to cry out when they are stepped on, but their cuticles, shells, and carapaces audibly express their protests. If we listen very carefully, these grinding pleas may reach our ears and our hearts. What if we could actually hear each life shriek under our feet? Perhaps our sanity depends on being selectively deaf. Maybe the Jain monks can hear these cries and that is why they walk barefoot and sweep the path. Once one has become even momentarily aware of this world beneath our feet, the voices are never completely silenced. When I traverse a prairie site filled with grasshoppers in the course of my work, I do not shed my shoes or sweep the insects ahead of me. But my pace and stride are changed for my experience. I walk more slowly, trying to give them a fair chance to avoid my falling feet. And I tend to shuffle a bit, dragging my toes to provide more disturbance in the grass—a sort of warning that I am coming through.

Arthropods have evolved hard exteriors, in part to protect their vulnerable interiors from the stumbling giants with whom they share the world. Humans have internal skeletons, but then we are rarely crushed. We have evolved into social creatures that are increasingly less likely to smash one another's skulls. Sociologists tell us that the murder rate in modern society is less than that at any time in our history, including our lengthy period as hunter-gatherers. But they've not considered the possibility that humans have simply replaced physical violence with psychological and spiritual violence. Insulting, disdaining, shunning, and slandering have largely replaced beatings, but the damage is no less severe. In response, we construct emotional shells to avoid the risks of intimacy—the heartbreak of failed relations, the harsh words of a supervisor, or the cruel judgment of a teacher. Our safe places shrink to the abstract confines of our own minds.

I'm protected by elaborate shells: the walls of a house, the steel of a car, the terms of an insurance policy, and the concrete of buildings—as if these barriers could keep my spirit from being crushed. Employers, co-workers, supervisors, leaders, and neighbors are moving so fast to secure the wealth needed to build their own shells that I fear being squashed beneath the wheels of progress. I'm like a snail, dragging my tiny sanctuary with me, afraid to overextend my soft and vulnerable being into the world. Society has become a giant, deaf to my cries and sure to crush me, despite my carefully contrived shell, if I dare move too slowly.

But I am coming to understand that if I hurry through life, then I also risk becoming a titan to my children, students, employees, and neighbors. In rushing to build my shell, it is easy to ignore the child, dismiss the student, overlook the employee, and forget the neighbor. As easily as a leather boot crushes a grasshopper on the prairie, thoughtless words can crush the spirit of a person. I can't avoid doing some harm or being hurt; walking barefoot means squashing a few fellow beings and flinching from the occasional thorn. However, I can slow down—at least a little, every so often. Moving at the pace of the naked sole on the prairie doesn't mean stopping, but it surely means causing less harm, both to myself and others.

I don't make a habit of walking barefoot on the prairie. More often, I remove my shoes for a stroll around the block, and there's something worthwhile in extending my stride just a tad to step over a pavement ant. Most often, I put on my shoes for an evening's amble with my wife, and there's something meaningful in extending our walk another few minutes to greet a neighbor. In either case—extending an inch or a moment—at least I've offered a reason for a fellow being to have a thinner shell. When we move more slowly and mindfully, our corner of the world is not just a different place. It's a better place.

Prayerful Science

When science is learned in love, and its powers are wielded by love, they will appear the supplements and continuations of the material creation.
—Ralph Waldo Emerson

I CONVERSE WITH GRASSHOPPERS. My earliest communication with these envoys of the prairie was through experimentation—the traditional means that a scientist uses to initiate a dialogue with the natural world. I would attempt to thin the number of grasshoppers on the range with judicious use of an insecticide. And then I'd listen for their reply. If my terms were too harsh, they replied with eerie silence, my words a lonely echo. Or sometimes they shouted their rebuttal, as in a study that I conducted several years ago.

Using stacks of old records, I listened for the grasshoppers' response to decades of our blanketing the grasslands with broad-spectrum insecticides. We had spoken loud and long, and the grasshoppers roared back with more frequent and severe outbreaks (it seems that we were wiping out their natural enemies). In response, we had used yet more insecticides in what become an ecological shouting match, without anyone taking the time to listen.

We've now developed methods that are more soft-spoken and there is hope of authentic, ecological dialogue. We may not have attained a quiet conversation yet, but at least the vitriolic argument of chemically intensive, large-scale programs and the outbursts of grasshopper populations in response appear to be over. This progress in our relationship with the land and its creatures through attentive science allows us to lower our voices and listen for replies. But it requires a novel approach to the world, one that has the elements of seeking both a new course of inquiry and a different way of being in the world.

An ecologist who wants to relate to a prairie as a living being worthy of deep respect is pushing the limits of modern science. I surely risk my professional credibility when I claim that I hear the creatures of the grasslands. Their speaking is neither literal nor metaphorical, but it is true in a way that transcends mere sensation and abstraction, reaching through and beyond the objective facts of ecology. What's more, I have learned to converse not only with the grasshoppers but the soil, grasses, and birds. I speak to the prairie and God answers. Well, sort of.

The notion of transcendent ecology implies a complex relationship with the divine that can be troubling for both conventional science and theology. In authentic dialogue, both parties are involved—and affected. And if God is perfect and complete, then what could be accomplished through engaging the Almighty? An omniscient, omnipotent God as a formulation of the divine seems impossibly distant and separate, like some sort of an oracle from which commands flow but into which nothing returns. Perhaps this difficulty is overcome with the notion of immanence, the greatest theological gift that Christianity has offered the world. The mythic power of Jesus was in his repudiation of dualism. The concept of God-made-flesh opened the door to the possibility, even the necessity, of scientifically informed theology—and divinely inspired science.

Religion and science can accommodate a reverent ecologist if *divine* is understood in the sense so beautifully developed by William James: that which is enveloping and real, to which the individual responds solemnly and tenderly. It seems possible for the ground of being to inform our insights and understandings, but at the same time to be reshaped by our questions and consequent actions. Pervasive and responsive, the "All" emerges, manifest at the scale of the cosmos and at the level of a blade of grass.

Perhaps my practice of reverent science is marginally tolerable if kept quiet. Such a notion is hardly the legitimate foundation for human inquiry regarding the natural world. There would seem to be potentially terrible costs of melding science and religion. Each has its role and place, but neither should be imposing itself on the other. But the hazards of excluding the divine from the scientific method are grave indeed. Without infusing scientific inquiry with meaning, we risk continued moral failure. Admittedly, ethics are not reducible to religious faith. On the other hand, spirituality has historically served as the most globally compelling basis for right living. Conversely, much of science is the pursuit of self-serving, personal curiosity with a primary devotion to professionalism and profitability. Wendell Berry argues that science (and art) has eroded into narcissism. He maintains that we have lost our moral bearings, our sense of propriety: "To raise the issue of propriety is to deny that any individual's wish is the ultimate measure of the world." There is a desperate need to see beyond our own desires, to imagine deeply what the world can be. This vision cannot be provided through an objective lens. According to Berry, "We know enough of our own history by now to be aware that people *exploit* what they have merely concluded to be of value, but they *defend* what they love."

For science to become a moral enterprise, it must subordinate itself to concerns that are larger than its own, concerns that cannot be heard without extending beyond its limits of rationalism. As an ecologist, I can and must take seriously the interdependence of lives. If I can truly perceive biotic communities (including farms) as enveloping and real, if I can respond to ecosystems (including cities) with solemnity and tenderness, then my science is infused with the divine. Reverent ecology requires perceiving the landscape as a Place—a setting where our lives become woven into the warp of the land and the woof of its inhabitants. Only in this way can I hope to refute Justice Holmes's contention that, "Science makes major contributions to minor needs. Religion, however small its successes, is at least at work on the things that matter most."

Reverence in the course of science serves as a pathway to authentic experience, which is the foundation of good research. To enter into dialogue with an abstraction, to speak and listen while engaging the "other" only in a theoretical sense, seems a bit pointless, even absurd. Hypothetical encounters with imaginary lovers seem unlikely to generate meaningful human experiences. Indeed, ecologists often deride the "desk jockey," the theoretician who models the natural world without ever having engaged the pasture or meadow that is converted into an equation or graph.

Reason is essential to science, but it is not sufficient for humanity. Houston Smith recounts the frustration of the Zen teacher who accuses his student of "philosopher's disease"—the compulsion to analyze and reduce the world to rational terms. But then the teacher reconsiders his own assessment of the student, saying, "However, reason can only work with the experience that is available to it. You obviously know how to reason. What you lack is the experience to reason wisely from. For these weeks put reason aside and work for experience." Like the Zen teacher, I can offer my students, who often are adept reasoners, the opportunity to speak to the prairie and listen to the voices of the land.

Ecology is a dialogue—a speaking and listening, not unlike prayer. Indeed, prayer might be most simply understood as a deliberate dialogue with the divine, a solemn and tender communication with enveloping reality. Whatever it is that the scientist finds ultimately real and that evokes authentic reflection—this is the divine. And surely this is both the jug that one fills and the well from which one draws, in quenching the thirst for meaning. In ecology, the prayerfulness of science is manifest in a dialogue with the land through its plant and animal emissaries. The key is for the ecologist to perceive the prairie—or stream or forest—as offering a primal reality, worthy of awe and admitting of reverence. Prayerful science recognizes that we have something to say to the world and, rather more provocatively, there will come a reply.

To practice ecology is to learn how to pray. The truly engaged and effective ecologist discovers a path to the divine. Perhaps the way is found in the course of a long hike to the headwaters of a rushing stream in a mountain clearing, a journey that becomes a pilgrimage to a "study site." Or it may become apparent during the ritual of a midday meal in the serenity of a forested cathedral, with databook, collecting vials, and pH meter set aside to make room for a reclining scientist. Or the ecologist might experience a kind of communion by plucking a grasshopper from a net, tenderly fanning its hindwings to reveal the crimson markings, gently tossing it into the perpetual breeze that strokes the prairie, and watching it disappear over a grassy hill. However it happens, the ecologist is guided into a dissolution of self, of permanence, of separateness from the world.

Inviting a prayerful approach to science might seem like inviting a divorced couple to an intimate dinner party—a very bad idea. After all, the separation of the sacred and the secular was a long and bitter battle. Galileo and Pope Urban VII or Charles Darwin and Bishop Wilberforce were not going to resolve their differences with a bit of counseling or mediation. But more than a century has passed, and I wonder whether the original arguments continue to resonate with the same ferocity. Suppose the differences were not irreconcilable—maybe rather than an annulment, science and religion have been going about their lives in a trial separation.

Science and religion once managed to find meaning in one another, in the days when natural history was viewed as a way to celebrate the Creation. The offspring of this union was sometimes a grotesque hybrid of perspectives, such as Isaac Newton's idea of God as a cosmic clock-maker. More often, the result was a beautiful blend of beliefs. The original text in my field is *An Introduction to Entomology*, published in 1815. In this text,

William Kirby and William Spence—referring to them-selves in the third person—explain their purpose:

> And here it may be proper to observe, that one of their first and favourite objects has been to direct the attention of their readers "from nature up to nature's God." . . . "*To see all things in God,*" has been accounted one of the peculiar privileges of a future state; and in this present life, "*to see God in all things,*" in the mirror of creation to behold and adore the reflected glory of the Creator, is no mean attainment; and it possesses this advantage, that thus we sanctify our pursuits, and, instead of lov-ing the creatures for themselves, are led by the survey of them and their instincts to the love of Him who made and endowed them.

Certainly no modern entomology text would offer students a theological rationale for the study of insects. But Konrad Lorenz, the "Father of Ethology," main-tained that, "without the love for the animal itself, no observer, however patient, could ever look at it long enough to make valuable observations on its behavior." He melded himself into the lives of the creatures who shared his grassy fields and, to his family's occasional dismay, his house. My graduate studies in entomology began with insect behavior, and Lorenz's wisdom continued to resonate as I moved into the field of ecology.

Love of a place or an animal, as Lorenz suggests, is a familiar act, although perhaps less so if the land is the austere steppe or the creature is the prosaic grasshopper. Ecological love is as much an act of humility as affection. The ecologist becomes mindfully connected to powers that he or she will never fully comprehend or control. Like the mind of a lover, a grassland is complex beyond our capacity to imagine, let alone understand. Lovers and lands are forever mysterious, but they can be engaged and explored, touched and tended. We can enter into dialogue, find the right questions to ask, and come to know more of them and ourselves.

Theologians tell us that prayer has myriad forms and functions. Upon returning to the grasslands after a winter of windchill and whiteness, I find myself engaged in a prayer of adoration. As I walk through the brief blush of green in late May, searching fervently for early grasshopper hatchlings to delineate our study sites, it feels good to stop and be still. There is a rightness in lapsing into moments of hushed reverence, becoming keenly aware of the Place.

Later, in the midst of the grasshoppers, prayer can take its purest form as contemplation. Especially in the lingering night-chilled morning or the tired, sweat-cooled hour of sunset, the grasshoppers become busy with their lives and I can see with the simplicity of a parent watching a child at play. There is no seeking, no wondering how, no asking why—only being with and among the creatures in a shared place of unspeakable meaning. This awareness is a form of spiritual objectivity, a paradoxical way of knowing in which separateness comes full circle to create connection. That is, by simply accepting whatever comes, I set myself aside, allowing nature to speak without translation, hearing the sum and substance of the world without preconception or judgment. In this profound way, objectivity becomes a form of ecstasy. This is not so etymologically absurd, as objectivity means "to perceive a separateness between self and other," and ecstasy means, quite literally, "to stand outside of." Good science and deep prayer become a matter of seeing the essence of the world.

Each year also brings death and yet another form of prayer. Much of our work involves developing safer and better ways of thinning grasshopper infestations on the rangeland. With pathogens and poisons, we attempt to find the means of keeping good stewards on the land while sustaining the natural cycles of insects, plants, soils, and water. And so a prayer of confession—admitting the harm that I do and conceding the unfathomable mystery that we must kill to live—seems essential.

The end of the season brings prayers of thanksgiving for whatever I have learned about myself, students, and grasshoppers—about the relationships that simultaneously place us within the land and embed the land within us. I am reminded of the grace said before a meal in preparation to consume the flesh of other creatures or the fruits of the earth. Because each year of research brings a portion of the understanding that is sought, along with unbidden gifts of insight, gratitude is proper.

The last prayer of the year is one that the rationalist might mock as the most common and foolish, the prayer of petition. This may be the most simple and complex act of supplication. I've come to understand that although this manner of praying seems least consistent with the institution of science, it is ultimately and irrevocably enmeshed with the life of the scientist. Finding myself in middle age, a time when injuries heal more slowly, muscles ache a bit longer, and illnesses seem to require more than passing attention, I am coming to understand that the scientist does not only wonder whether a line of inquiry is worth living for but whether it is worth dying for. Each passing day is an irretrievable gift, and to squander this blessing on the heartless, soulless interrogation of nature would be to offer oneself as a martyr to the cult of objectivity. So, how does a scientist discover a question or a topic worthy of investigation? The same way that humans have sought insight and inspiration for millennia—through prayer. If I realize the finitude and depth of my existence, and if I understand that each day is an irrecoverable and mysterious gift, then how could I, as a scientist, fail to pray in search of a question that is worthy of my life?

As a student, I was taught that the power of science lies in its commitment to the ideal of objectivity. The goal was to design, conduct, analyze, and interpret experiments with absolutely dispassionate, uncontaminated reason. In light of the standard "experiments" conducted in the requisite college biology, chemistry, and physics laboratories, this was philosophically correct, but operationally bad, advice. The student who managed to apparently create matter (an impossible but common outcome of syntheses in organic chemistry, thanks to mis-measured reactants and worn-out scales) was not rewarded for objective reporting. No praise was offered to the budding geneticist who supposedly refuted Mendelian inheritance (a most unlikely but frequent result with fruit flies, due to the skewed ratios arising as winged ones escaped and wingless ones became mired in their gooey food). However, we understood that in the course of "real" science, one had to adhere to the ideal of objectivity with uncompromising devotion.

The problem with this approach to education was that once I became a professional scientist, nobody was handing me a lab manual full of preconceived experiments. I was hired as an insect ecologist at the University of Wyoming to explore the world of grasshoppers, with a particular eye toward managing populations of these creatures when they became unruly. In graduate school, my research had been quasi-independent, guided by a gentle mentor and a thoughtful committee. As a new faculty member, I relished the lack of supervision—but freedom is scary stuff. I discovered that the most important and difficult phase of science is asking a good question. Our ignorance is such a boundless resource (at least in ecology), that one must attempt to navigate through a mindscape of tangled paths, blind alleys, twisted streets, and unsigned roads. I had learned the principles of objectively designing experiments, impartially collecting data, rigorously analyzing the results, and neutrally interpreting their meaning. I knew how to answer questions using science, but standing in the midst of a few million grasshoppers milling about on the mixed-grass prairie, I realized that generating results was the easy part of science. The hard part was answering the question, "What should I ask?"

The first and most critical step of science is to find, select, hear, or otherwise discover a question that ought to be answered. I recall one of my graduate-school mentors noting that there are plenty of people who can generate correct answers through science but few who can ask the right questions. In this defining phase of inquiry, the ideal of objectivity not only fails to provide guidance, it becomes an absurd—if not utterly impossible—standard. I've sometimes wondered what it would be like for a scientist to select questions in a purely dispassionate, utterly disconnected manner. Many scientists approximate this condition in pursuing topics that are deemed important by the collective consciousness of their peers in a socially sanctioned, positive-feedback system that provides comfort and security. But this effort to become the lead sheep in the flock (an odd but perhaps apt metaphor) lacks an objective rationale. Some scientists use the standard of "publishability" and choose the questions that are most likely to yield manuscripts, and still others select the measure of "fundability" and focus on those matters most likely to yield grants. Of course, any of these approaches risks the pitfall of infinite regress in a scientific version of the theological quandary, "who made the maker of the universe?" That is, the very process of selecting the supposedly objective criterion—peer approval, publication, or funding—is an act loaded with subjectivity. Perhaps the only possible approach would be to construct a database of all possible scientific questions and then to select one randomly for examination. Such silliness simply reflects the absurdity of the claim that science is a purely objective venture.

I could not possibly have devoted seventeen years of my working life to the study of grasshopper ecology without a passion for these creatures and the lessons they offer about the grasslands. Even taking out time for teaching, meeting, and other duties of academia, I've spent a bit more than two thousand working days—nine years of full-time work—trying to understand these ambassadors of the range. No sane person would devote such labor, let alone so much of one's life, to the pursuit of questions that did not touch the heart and soul while stimulating the mind. To have invested that much of life is either a tragic waste of human potential or an expression of faith in the mysteries and lessons worthy of this expenditure. And so, at the end of each summer field-season my prayerful petition is for an answer to the question, "What am I to do next year as a scientist?" I trust that the answer will come slowly, from unexpected teachers, in unanticipated ways, over the course of the long winter.

Ralph Waldo Emerson provided us with one of the most timeless warnings about modern life:

> The gods we worship write their names on our faces, be sure of that. And a man will worship something—have no doubt about that, either. He may think that his tribute is paid in secret in the dark recesses of his heart—but it will out. That which dominates will determine his life and character. Therefore, it behooves us to be careful what we worship, for what we are worshiping we are becoming.

I wonder, however, whether this lofty warning grew from humble origins. Years before, Emerson had en-

gaged in a memorable conversation with a common laborer named Tarbox. This simple man explained that
men are always praying, and that all prayers are granted.
With this uncomplicated interpretation of spirituality,
the laborer revealed that we are constantly engaged in
shaping the world through our desires, wishes, fears,
and hopes. Emerson listened, the great mind of the minister understanding the great heart of the laborer. "We
must beware then," Emerson concluded, "what we ask."

In the end, it might be argued, everyone prays—
laborers, ministers, even scientists. Perhaps we all petition the divine in some manner. The difference, if such
exists, is that the scientist prays for questions, rather
than answers.

The Good Hunt

To hunt tigers one must have a brother's help.
—Chinese proverb

BURNT ORANGE SHAG CARPET, dark simulated-wood paneling, and tiny, lather-free bars of soap—this was home on the range. At least it has been a home away from home for my field crew and me since 1995. *The Western* is an L-shaped, twenty-room, park-in-front-of-your-door, circa 1950s motel. Simple, cheap, old, and—the reason we stay there—managed by two of the kindest people on earth. Come spring, John and Joyce treat us like the returning swallows of Capistrano. All summer long, John knows when the guys can be expected back from a day on Wyoming's sere grasslands, and he turns on the rumbling air conditioners so the rooms are cool when they arrive. Even after a day of failed hunting, Joyce's motherly delight in seeing our trucks pull into the parking lot puts life back in perspective.

Although Torrington erected a rather elegant statue of giant pheasants on the highway into town as a means of enticing hunters, our quarry was rather more prosaic. We were hunting grasshoppers—not individual insects but an entire population comprising what we referred to as a "good" infestation (good for our studies, not so good for the rancher). We needed several hundred acres of prairie with about twenty grasshoppers per square yard. A patch of a hundred million grasshoppers or so would be just the ticket to get us started laying out plots for the summer's research. But we hadn't found our quarry.

It would seem that hunting something that covered a couple of square miles should have been fairly easy, but there are forty-three hundred square miles in Platte and Goshen counties. We've come to know this land, having rambled over the region for a couple of months every year over the course of nearly two decades. You see a lot of a place while racking up a hundred thousand miles on dirt roads. Because we work in pairs, you also see a whole bunch of the other guys in the crew. We'd spent the equivalent of an entire year together in the cab of a pickup, a prolonged intimacy that many marriages could not withstand. But even this intensity of hunting didn't assure us of finding our quarry.

Grasshoppers don't make themselves obvious in an explosion of feathered flight like pheasants, nor do they poke their heads up and create stunning silhouettes at dusk, like deer. To find grasshoppers, however, requires some of the same tactics as hunting bigger game. An experienced grasshopper hunter knows the best spots (look near gently rising, south-facing, sandy slopes), uses years of experience (the edges of the Goshen Hole, and the grasslands surrounding 66 Mountain are good bets), tucks away quasi-superstitious natural patterns (a row of lark buntings on a strand of barbed wire means that high densities of grasshoppers are in the area), and catches tips from the locals (according to Dean, the Teeter's place out by Lingle was overrun with grasshoppers last summer, and Steve said that Sandy ran into a terrible mess of grasshoppers near Canyon View Ranch). Hunting is a bridge, formed by the quarry and spanning the gap between people and places. There's a reason why hunting and fishing guides, people who know the land and its creatures, dramatically improve the success of their clients. And there's a reason why some local folks consider guided hunts a bit like one-night stands, lacking in the protracted period of courtship and struggle that makes for a genuine and lasting relationship.

Today's failure, however, was probably more a matter of bad timing than being in the wrong place. We usually get out a bit too early in the spring, before the grasshoppers have started to hatch in earnest. Our official excuse is that we need to find "good" infestations before summer arrives because the window of opportunity for our research program in grasshopper control is very narrow. This past year, we had three weeks to pull together the logistics for treating forty-two plots of forty acres (about as many football fields in size) with ground and aerial applications of three insecticides and an insect pathogen, in solid and liquid formulations. But the real reason for our too-early ventures into the field is that laboratory fever sets in about April, when the long Wyoming winter begins to lose its grip and for the next month or two spring seems to be just around the corner.

These unsuccessful hunts are a chance to return to a familiar land and renew conversations with my friends and students about the coming season, grasshoppers, weather, sports, hobbies, and life. This is my homecoming, having all of the elements needed to knit together a place—good land, good times, and good friends.

Returning to this corner of Wyoming is surely not most people's view of exciting travel to an exotic locale. My bookkeeper at the University suggested that an auditor's eyebrows might be raised by the number of meals and nights of lodging that we claim, but if there's ever any question she will, "just send the auditor to Torrington for a week and that'll convince anyone that you're not there on vacation." The land is harsh—hot, dry, and empty. Unlike western Wyoming's picturesque Jackson Hole, the defining feature of this land is the Goshen Hole, a 680-square mile, wind-scoured depression in the earth that grades into the desolate sandhills of Nebraska, as if a cosmic cow had left a hundred-foot-deep hoofprint.

Nor is our field work high adventure or stimulating science. We spend our days bouncing along in pickups (not National Geographic-funded dugout canoes or camel caravans), walking across shortgrass prairie (not the romantic tall grass of the Midwest or the vibrant jungles of the Amazon) to catch and count grasshoppers (not radio-collared wolves or breaching whales). Our lunch staple is Wheat Thin crackers, and we start our day at six in the morning with Mini Mart coffee. And we don't run the air conditioner during the day for two reasons. First, only one of the trucks has this luxury, so it doesn't seem fair to use it when the other guys are sweltering. Second, using this extravagant technology generates a devastating thermal shock to your system in the course of repeatedly moving from the artificially cool cab into the hundred-degree heat and back again.

Nor are we most people's idea of great company. We consider a debate on the best strategy for crossing a three-strand barbed wire fence to be fine conversation— the resolution being a complex matter of how tightly the fence is strung, the proximity of support posts, the height and weight of the individual making the crossing, and the slope of the land under the fence. Nobody in the field crew is particularly witty or urbane, and we only know a couple of dozen jokes among us. Our lives are awfully normal, with gardening, fishing, camping, and home repairs being standard fare for discussion. But these guys are genuine and decent. They might not be entertaining at a cocktail party or gallery opening but if your car broke down on the way home, they'd stop and offer you a ride. And you'd probably accept their offer because they come across as the sort of people you can trust.

Back at *The Western* after a dinner of chicken-fried steak, I clicked on the television and surfed through all forty-five channels on cable. Nothing. Even ESPN and the History Channel were duds this evening. So, I dug out my reading material, one of the books that I'd chosen for my class on "Great Books of the Life Sciences," a course that was a blissful escape into pure academics with interesting and motivated students. My dog-eared copy of *Walden* was highlighted in three different colors, with penciled notes in the margins. Finding my favorite passages was easy, and this evening I sought Henry David Thoreau's insights regarding hunting. Before a season of killing, it is good to hear the blessings and admonitions of sages. Thoreau, the patron saint of environmentalists, maintained, "There is a period in the history of the individual, as of the race, when the hunters are the 'best men,' as the Algonquins called them. We cannot but pity the boy who has never fired a gun; he is no more human, while his education has been sadly neglected."

While growing up, boys often hunt birds or rabbits. I hunted lizards. At least, that's what my older brother, Steve, and I called our forays into the fields behind our house in Albuquerque. In 1970, our folks had built a new house at the edge of the city, bordering a sparse, desert grassland freckled with cacti and lined with tumbleweed-choked dry washes. For some reason, the locals call this habitat "mesa"—a term normally reserved for the distinctive flat-topped landforms of the Southwest. Our potential hunting grounds stretched almost uninterrupted from the edge of our yard to the Sandia mountains, but our operational range encompassed a couple of hundred acres—or the distance from which our mother could still see us when she looked over the back wall.

We had no tradition of "real" hunting or fishing in our family, although our parents enjoyed the outdoors, often taking us and our two younger siblings picnicking in the summer and skiing in the winter. My only memory of blood sport was a day of fishing in the ocean with my uncle when we visited relatives in Connecticut; I caught a puffer fish and Steve landed a tomcod. This outing aroused my hunting instinct. But as there were no enduring adult models to foster this primal behavior, I have to conclude that my desire to stalk and seize other creatures was innate.

In retrospect, it seems that our lizard hunts met several needs, the most superficial of which was financial.

After a day's hunt, we delivered our live quarry to the pet stores for payment. Bluetails were worth twenty-five cents, and sanddiggers netted us a dime. This seemed fair, given that catching a bluetail was by far the more difficult venture, involving a wild series of flush-and-chase bouts across the field, while the sanddiggers often made only a brief dash before attempting to avoid detection by squirming into a patch of hot dust. But this difference was almost surely not the source of the pricing scheme. Although I wasn't entirely sure what the pet stores did with the lizards, I gathered that a few were sold as pets but most served as snake food. The larger bluetails probably brought a higher price because they were a more substantial serpent snack. Sometimes I wonder if our mom didn't have a deal worked out with the neighborhood pet store to assure a market for the lizards, as our hunting expeditions kept us extremely busy, reasonably safe, and out of her hair for hours during summer vacation. A good day's catch would be perhaps ten lizards, which might yield $2.20. Split between us, this worked out to be about eighteen cents an hour. Even for an eleven-year-old kid, the economic returns couldn't justify the effort.

The greater payoff for lizard hunting ran far deeper than financial profits. The thrill of the hunt was in our blood. Heading out across the mesa, I could feel the adrenalin leaking into my veins, and the call of "There's one!" opened the floodgates. We were armed with a red, plastic bucket rather than a rifle, but any full-fledged hunter would have identified with our heightened sense of anticipation, keenness of vision, and intensity of focus.

We developed a rather sophisticated system. Catching lizards is like fishing, where perhaps 80 percent of the fish will be found in 20 percent of the stream. If one doesn't know where to cast, hours can pass without a nibble. So we learned where lizards hide. They'd bask in open areas in the early morning, but for most of the day they sought shade from the New Mexican heat. Scraps of cardboard and other refuse that blew in from surrounding construction sites made ideal shelters.

We had well-defined roles in the chase. Steve would lift one edge of the debris, while I stood about ten feet behind him. We'd discovered that a lizard would either bolt away from him, in which case he could give immediate chase, or it would dash at him, zipping between his legs. This latter event led to many lost lizards in our early hunts when I stood on the opposite side of the debris facing my brother. So we developed the "shotgun formation" of a football lineup, with Steve bent over like a center and me standing as if ready to receive the snap of the ball. From this position, I could intercept the lizards that chose to run past him.

Once a lizard was flushed from cover, the nearest hunter cried out and gave chase. Sometimes, a lizard would disappear down a rodent hole or into an impenetrable jumble of dried tumble weed, and the hunt was over. But more often, the lizard would sprint for ten or twenty yards and dive into a clump of grass or cactus. Then we took up our positions, with Steve attempting to make the catch and me assuring that we would not lose our quarry if it bolted again. The process was repeated, with the lizard making shorter dashes as it tired.

Catching the lizard was the climax of the hunt, and this required special skill. Bluetails use autotomy as a defense—their tails break off when grabbed. The writhing tail is an effective diversionary tactic, giving the lizard time to escape. The pet stores might begrudgingly accept tailless lizards, but we felt that this was a sign of a sloppy hunt—the equivalent of a gut-shot deer. A truly competent lizard hunter should be able to secure his quarry intact, and Steve rarely failed in this regard. Lacking the finesse and confidence to make sure-handed captures, I was only allowed to handle the lizards once they were safely inside the bucket. I can still remember the feel of their supple, paper-thin, leathery skin and the prick of the tiny needles at the ends of their elongated toes. To catch a lizard, one must come to know the life and land of the lizards, but perhaps my ultimate purpose was to know my brother.

Steve is three years older than I am. And I admired, enraged, venerated, teased, and loved him in the unspoken way of a brother. He was brilliant and strong, and he set a high standard for me. I probably would have been a lazy student and a half-hearted athlete had it not been for his example. Steve adored competition; he whipped me in tennis, basketball, football (a creative one-on-one version), and board games. I secretly hated competing against him, but I loved playing with him. I wanted to be on his team, but without other kids in our newly built neighborhood it was difficult to find ways to be his teammate. Lizard hunting created the chance to compete against a common and worthy opponent, to objectively assess our performance in terms of an external standard, to win or lose together. I'm not sure what aroused my brother's passion for the hunt. Steve had horrible allergies, and on the mesa his eyes would redden and nearly swell shut; some afternoons, he seemed to nearly drown in mucous, blowing his nose for long minutes to clear his head. But he never complained, and we never cut a hunting trip short for his sake. Something made it worth his suffering.

A few years ago, Steve came up to Wyoming with his family for a visit. He is a conservative, atheistic rationalist who bikes avidly, avoids fat, and plays to win; I am a liberal, theistic mystic who writes essays, likes butter, and plays for fun. But we're brothers, so we abandoned the wives and kids for a day and went fishing on Big Creek, a gorgeous stretch of river that has cut a sagebrush-lined canyon into the prairie near the Colorado border. I knew more about fishing than he did, but he quickly mastered the basics of casting and soon read the water well enough to find the fish. As we stood together on the banks of a deep, still curve of the river, one of us hooked what must have been a five-pound rainbow trout. The rod bent double and the line whipped through the water just before the fish exploded from the depths, danced across the surface, and broke free. It's odd that I can remember our jubilant cries during the fight, our wail of disappointment in losing the fish, and then our joyous laughter at the spectacle of having encountered such a wonderful creature—but I honestly can't remember who hooked the fish. I think it was me, but the experience was so intimately shared that the memory would not be diminished for me if I learned that the fisherman was my brother.

Now I spend my days hunting grasshoppers, an even more unusual quarry than lizards. I like the work—it is meaningful and important. Our research has yielded dramatic reductions in pesticide use and helped good ranchers stay on the land. I say "our" because there are always a half dozen of us working together. Scott has been with me the longest, ten years, and I don't know if I'd keep to my current line of work if he wasn't with me to recount previous years, share in the hunt, and plan future forays. We've spent a lot of time together, and we constantly talk over new ideas for thinning grasshopper populations to levels that sustain the prairie and the people, along with discussing home repairs, university politics, world affairs, and a slew of other subjects. What we ultimately share are places, sculpted from the grasslands through our mutual experience of the hunt.

But some topics we avoid. I don't think we'd agree on party politics, and there's not much talk about personal relationships or religion. Our culture supposes that these latter topics would be shared in a deep friendship, but I wonder if such discussions aren't sometimes a ritual between people who must display to themselves and one another a certain vulnerability to assure that an authentic relationship exists. I don't particularly desire heart-wrenching, soul-baring conversations with Scott. I prefer the simple joy of being in the presence of a person who I know and trust, in the presence of a land that knows our silent story. Our mutual respect and admiration goes unspoken, as it should when actions make such personal matters clear.

In hunting for grasshopper infestations in Wyoming, I don't encounter any lizards, but the treeless landscape evokes memories. I savor the bliss of friendship and endure the pang that arises unbidden from my childhood. The mesa behind our parents' house is now covered in apartment buildings, stores, and parking lots. Steve and I both have had knee surgery, so careening across the uneven desert grassland in pursuit of a lizard would probably be a bad idea in any case. His allergies are finally under control after a long series of injections, but mine have developed in the past few years. I think our lizard hunting days are over, but I hope we fish again—together.

Our lives are stories. Shakespeare was right when he penned, "All the world's a stage, And all the men and women merely players." The play that is my life involves plot, setting, and characters. The best acts are those in which these elements come together, reinforcing one another. Perhaps it is tragic that many of the most meaningful scenes have hunting as the plot, sparse landscapes as the setting, and a brother-friend as the character. But the purpose of the Greek tragedy was to ask questions about human nature, wonder about our place in the universe, and explore the relation between ourselves and the powers that govern life. I know of no better place for a tragedy than the grasslands.

Sanctuary

We cannot dedicate, we cannot consecrate, we cannot hallow this ground. The brave men, living and dead, who struggled here, have consecrated it far above our poor power to add or detract.
—Abraham Lincoln

As I HIKE AWAY from the rim of the canyon formed by the Yellowstone River, the thundering falls and thronging sightseers, give way to murmuring breezes and teeming grasshoppers. Tourists come to Yellowstone National Park to see the fiery underworld—steaming fumaroles, seething mud pots, and roaring geysers. I am hoping to find an aspect of nature far more rare and ephemeral, a spark of life that has not flamed for a hundred years. I seek the creature that once irrupted from this land to blacken the skies. From here it periodically spread over the continent, covering a region even larger than the area dusted by the ash that spewed six hundred thousand years ago from the Yellowstone caldera—a fifty mile-long crater formed during the largest volcanic eruption in the history of North America. I am looking for the last refuge of the Rocky Mountain locust.

During its outbreaks, the Rocky Mountain locust (a locust being a particular type of grasshopper that reaches tremendous population densities and forms swarms) could be found in an area stretching from Canada to Mexico and from California to Iowa. In the *Second Report of the U.S. Entomological Commission*, I came across an account of a swarm that staggers the imagination and bested the old record (a desert locust swarm over Africa) by a thousand-fold. According to the first-hand account of Dr. Albert Lyman Child, a swarm of Rocky Mountain locusts passed over Plattsmouth, Nebraska, in 1875. By timing the rate of movement as the insects streamed overhead for five days and by telegraphing to surrounding towns, he was able to estimate that the swarm was 1,800 miles long and at least 110 miles wide. Based on his information, this swarm covered a swath equal to the combined areas of Connecticut, Delaware, Maine, Maryland, Massachusetts, New Hampshire, New Jersey, New York, Pennsylvania, Rhode Island, and Vermont. This record-setting swarm would have included more than a trillion locusts—500 times greater than the human population of the planet. If we allow that each individual weighed about half of a gram, then the swarm would have outweighed a human by the same magnitude that a whale outweighs a mouse.

Throughout the nineteenth century, swarms of locusts regularly turned noon into dusk, devastating farm communities and bringing trains to a halt as the crushed bodies of the insects greased the rails. Laura Ingalls Wilder's stories of pioneer life are woven in the fabric of American culture, and perhaps no account better portrays the Rocky Mountain locust than these lines from *On the Banks of Plum Creek*:

> The light was queer. It was not like the changed light before a storm. The air did not press down as it did before a storm. Laura was frightened, she did not know why... The cloud was hailing grasshoppers. The cloud was grasshoppers. Their bodies hid the sun and made darkness. Their thin, large wings gleamed and glittered. The rasping whirring of their wings filled the whole air and they hit the ground and the house with the noise of a hailstorm ... In bed, Laura and Mary could still hear the whirring and snipping and chewing. Laura felt

the claws crawling on her. There were no grasshoppers in bed, but she could not brush the feeling off her arms and cheeks. In the dark she saw grasshoppers' bulging eyes and felt their claws until she went to sleep. . . . [In the morning] the whole prairie had changed. The grasses did not wave; they had fallen in ridges. The willow trees were bare. In the plum thickets only a few plumpits hung to the leafless branches. The nipping, clicking, gnawing sound of the grasshoppers' eating was still going on . . . .

It is no wonder that these locusts were considered "the single greatest impediment to the settlement of the western states." Today, we can barely imagine the immense herds of bison or vast swarms of locusts that flowed over the land. But if we find it difficult to visualize such masses of life, it is even more challenging to grasp that less than thirty years after Wilder's account, the Rocky Mountain locust disappeared forever. Never again would this continent witness an eerie shadow sweeping across the cloudless prairie giving way to the papery rattle of billions of insects in flight. Such events are still known on every other inhabited landmass, but the people of the Great Plains can no longer experience a biological eclipse of the sun.

In most years, the climatic factors necessary to elicit an outbreak of the Rocky Mountain locust did not develop, and their populations eked out a living restricted to the fertile river valleys of the West. In the late 1800s, the pioneers transformed these areas. Many of these ecosystems were converted into farmland, cattle and sheep were introduced, beavers were eliminated along with their troublesome dams, and the streams were diverted for irrigation. The agriculturalists managed to inadvertently destroy the locusts' refuges, driving their most severe competitors to extinction in a matter of a few years. The last living specimen of the Rocky Mountain locust was caught in 1902.

The only locust habitat to survive this human onslaught was the Yellowstone River valley. Yellowstone was established as a National Park in 1872, when the Rocky Mountain locust was in its heyday. So the protected river valley in this park represents the most viable potential refuge for a remnant population of the Rocky Mountain locust. With only a single generation per year, the locust did not have time to evolve in response to the changes wrought by the pioneers. This species had an ecological taproot thousands of years old anchoring it to a land that had been swept away by the onslaught of human progress.

For a species to become wholly reliant on a place or a habitat requires that it sacrifice other options, accepting the risks of being profoundly and deeply linked to a landscape. When in the course of evolution such an ecological setting is found, the species comes to flourish in this place. For the Rocky Mountain locust, the fertile river valleys of the West represented a sanctuary, a habitat where they could always find what they needed to persist in the face of adversity. For the human species there are also such places, sociobiological habitats that comprise less than a millionth of the Earth's surface but through which nearly three-quarters of all people pass several times a year—our churches, mosques, synagogues, and temples.

The concept of the *sacred* is rooted in the same etymological origin as *sacrifice*, which is an act that engenders holiness through loss, suffering, denial, or pain. Holiness, in turn, is a special condition that is associated with transcendent meaning, so that a place of sacrifice is imbued with importance greater than its physical context. In Western society, we avoid sacrifice and seek security, comfort, and pleasure. However, we continue to struggle with the nature, meaning, and necessity of suffering. And so we often recount stories of sacrifice in our places of worship. In a reciprocal way, places of momentous loss often become sacred, such as battlefields at Gettysburg and Little Big Horn, the Edmund Pettus Bridge in Selma, the North Bridge in Concord, or a simple roadside cross adorned with flowers.

We also honor places of sanctuary where we have found safety amidst a world of turmoil and trouble, such as the hiding place of Anne Frank, Thoreau's cabin site at Walden Pond, or our childhood homes. Perhaps our most sacred spaces both remind us of suffering and offer us sanctuary. But what of other species? Does sacrifice or sanctuary define the extraordinary places in their lives? Do these places need to be consciously and intentionally chosen, or can a sacred space emerge in the context of evolution and ecology?

We are reluctant to call the habitats of other species sacred because their sacrifices are not intentional and their seeking of sanctuary is unconscious. But we did not plan for a grassy knoll in Dallas to be the place where we would lose President Kennedy; we did not intend for a buck-and-rail fence east of Laramie to be the site where Matthew Shepard would be sacrificed to our fear of differences; and we did not design the basements and attics of the houses along the underground railroad to be sanctuaries for runaway slaves. On the tenth of September, 2001, the World Trade Center was simply a gigantic office building, the Pentagon was just another government facility, and a reclaimed strip mine in Shanksville, Pennsylvania, was only a vacant lot. Nobody could have imagined the losses that would utterly transform the meaning of these places.

As self-aware animals, we do what we can to honor and protect our sacred spaces, and perhaps we should not deny other creatures their own ways of knowing and keeping deeply valued places. All species have stories of suffering and sanctuary in ecological and evolutionary times. To have survived in this world is to have risked, lost, groped, huddled, and grasped according to our abilities. These stories and places of loss and triumph are encoded in all beings; are they less real or less important if they are not maintained by thought or word?

The Rocky Mountain locust, the Native Americans, and the early European settlers of the West found that the serene and lush river valleys provided fresh water, abundant food, and reliable protection from severe weather. Each made sacrifices and probably fought to establish their hold on these fertile grasslands, and each understood that these havens would provide a sanctuary in times of difficulty. The locust sacrificed the sedentary life of the grasshopper—a stable, safe, and mundane existence—for the chance to periodically transform its life into one of delirious exuberance. Levels of abundance that we can barely imagine signaled the locust's wings to extend, its color to darken, and its movements to intensify in preparation for the ecstatic swarms.

As with the Native Americans whose cultures eroded with their displacement from sacred lands, the Rocky Mountain locust could not change fast enough to adapt to alternative sanctuaries. The complex and intimate connections between the land and native species are difficult—perhaps impossible—to express in objective, scientific terms, but sacred places are central to the well-being of many creatures. Even with all of the "right" conditions of temperature, light, humidity, and diet, animals often languish in zoos. They are unable to express what is missing and perhaps we would be unable to understand, unless we too had experienced the soul-wrenching loss of being forced from a farm or ranch that had been in the family for generations or being driven from a homeland that defined our traditions, stories, and hopes.

What if I find a pocket of habitat still harboring the Rocky Mountain locust? Regulatory officials might well advocate their destruction to avoid a return to the swarms of the 1800s. However, in my fantasy scenario, I like to imagine that in an ironic twist of logic, economic entomologists point out that pest is a label that can be applied only under appropriate conditions of population density. That is, a population of Rocky Mountain locusts that has not bothered us for a century could hardly be termed pests, as they have not attained outbreak levels. From the environmental camp, a few voices might call for protecting these insects as important components of a native ecosystem that is struggling to sustain biotic integrity. Some might argue that the Rocky Mountain locust serves as a reminder that we must share this world with other species (even those that we have not tamed or controlled). And a few advocates probably would invoke the powerful place of this species in the story of the West and the folklore of America. Sadly, the insect could not count on the vaunted Endangered Species Act. There is no political asylum for locusts; the law exempts pests from protection.

Among the grasshoppers that I collect from Yellowstone National Park, one female has spectacularly long wings. Females are very difficult to identify, but she is officially recorded as *Melanoplus bruneri*, the same genus as the Rocky Mountain locust but not the same species. I may be wrong in my classification of that long-winged female, but mistaken identities can sometimes be a saving grace for unwelcome individuals. Later, I capture several similar individuals from a meadow, although they lack the ventral yellow coloration that is typical of *M. bruneri*. I think I know who they are, so I release them back into the field. Because I do not remove them from the Park, their identities and location need not be reported to the authorities.

Some sanctuaries only persist in secret.

Becoming Native

One portion of land is the same to him as the next,
for he is a stranger who comes in the night
and takes from the land whatever he needs.
The earth is not his brother, but his enemy,
and when he has conquered it, he moves on.
—Chief Seattle

IT SEEMS THAT EVERY TIME I move to a new place, I feel crummy. Moving from New Mexico to Louisiana for graduate studies was miserable, and even moving from Wyoming to Australia and Vermont for sabbatical leaves left me with a sense of bodily malaise, diffuse anxiety, and vague disconnectedness—a sort of physical, mental, and spiritual dyspepsia. Of course, I soon recover and settle into my new surroundings, and life takes on a sense of normalcy. But no matter how much I relish the adventure of travel, the excitement of being in a different setting, and the potential of fresh relationships, I inevitably suffer through the first days. Conversely, when I leave these adopted contexts and return to the place that I perceive as "home," I never experience distress. Returning to the Laramie Valley feels good. More than that, it feels right. Maybe the grasslands are meant to be my home. Perhaps one's home—the place that is right—can be known through body, mind, and soul.

Genuine health is somehow tied to a sense of being rooted in a place, a homeland. In this context, we place great value on being *native*, but what does this really mean? Most often, we use this term to refer to those who were first to occupy a landscape. The native people are those who initially settled in a region. The term *first Americans* is at least half right; these people's ancestors were here "first," although it wasn't "America" when they arrived. Likewise, I've heard a United Nations attorney for native peoples refer to his clients as the *first nations*, a term that may be legally compelling but imposes upon these cultures a political-legal context that seems wholly inappropriate. I suspect, however, that he was using the law to protect native people in the same way that conservationists (myself included) often use economic arguments to protect native species—doing the right thing for the wrong reason is a popular approach in the modern world. In any case, it is the notion of "first" that seems to matter.

Unfortunately, this notion of being first becomes problematic in both practice and principle. During a fellowship in New Zealand, where I was attempting to help sort out the effects of some introduced insects, I learned a bit about the native people. Contrary to popular notions, the Maori were not the first humans on the islands. The original inhabitants were the Moriori, peaceful hunter-gatherers who were eliminated by the more aggressive Maoris. So, the native people of New Zealand appear to have attained their status by virtue of genocide. In principle, too, the "finders keepers" approach to the world seems flawed, even a bit adolescent. Surely there is more to the notion of being native than a series of largely accidental human invasions in which the first people call "dibs!" on the land. By looking backwards to define ourselves, we become locked in the conflicts of history, as the Middle East and Eastern Europe have. Søren Kierkegaard was right: "Life is understood backwards but must be lived forwards."

While chasing grasshoppers on the grasslands of Inner Mongolia several years ago, I had the good fortune to be invited into the mud-walled home of a local herdsman. Following a morning of bone-jarring jaunts across the landscape in a jeep without any suspension, the promise of a quiet meal was very welcome. After three weeks in China, I was missing my family, and as I watched the man's wife preparing lunch I was overwhelmed by a sense of being home—not my house in Wyoming but my childhood home in New Mexico. The woman's profile—widely set ebony eyes embedded in a flat, weather-worn face of quiet dignity—and her strong, heavy body wrapped in a shawl of coarse wool were those of the Navajo. The smell of hot oil and the taste of fried bread were precisely the sensations that I knew from thirty years earlier. This woman was so similar to the Indians of New Mexico that it seemed that the first North Americans might have crossed the Bering Strait within my lifetime. Rather than Native Americans, the Indians of my youth suddenly became Mongolian Americans. It seems to me that we must let history be our teacher, not our master. Perhaps it is time, now that all of the earth's landscapes are occupied or otherwise claimed, to create the future not solely in terms of the past. We are all from "somewhere else."

In college, I had a friend who used to check the "Native American" box on various forms even though he was a European mongrel like myself. He contended that he was born here, so he was native. Technically, he was right. The term *native* is derived from the Latin *natus*, the participle form of "to be born." In this sense, most people in the United States are native Americans. And surely one's place of birth is relevant to defining and understanding oneself. I always chuckle at the old story about a eulogy for a fellow who died in Maine at the age of ninety-seven. The minister noted, "We'll miss Bob as 'one of our own,' even though he wasn't native to these parts, having moved here with his family when he was two years old."

But equating being born in a place with being native doesn't seem quite right in the modern world. A few years ago, in response to the Maine-like tendency to give special standing based on literal nativity, folks in Wyoming started sporting bumper stickers on their trucks that declared, "Wyomingite by choice, not accident of birth." In today's mobile world, where you are born may have more to do with your parents' travels, the location of medical facilities, and the vagaries of employment opportunities than a meaningful tie to the land or a human community. I was born in Connecticut, but I am no more a Yankee than Edward Abbey was Pennsylvanian or John Muir was Scottish.

As I discovered in teaching a course on biodiversity at the University of Wyoming, being born in a region does not necessarily give one much understanding of the land. For several years, my co-instructor and I conducted a survey of students, mostly freshmen and sophomore non-science majors, in which we asked them to name three plants, vertebrates, and invertebrates that were native to this state. About 80 percent of the students were from Wyoming, and given the penchant of our citizens to hunt, fish, and camp, it seemed fair to expect that the students would be able to name some of their biological neighbors. We were reasonable in our interpretations of their answers, accepting common names such as "lodgepole pine" but not vague terms such as "pine tree." Year after year, the results were similar—and disturbing. Only about a third of the students from Wyoming could name even one native plant, about a quarter could name a native vertebrate, and less than one in twenty could name a native invertebrate. Nativity via birth seems to confer little of what we value when we refer to the virtues of being native.

Naming, whether applied to other creatures or ourselves, is a powerful way of relating to the world. Sloppy language is often evidence of sloppy thinking. And so we ought to name our valued concepts with great care. It seems that *Native American* does not really touch on the qualities that I treasure. The essence of the under-lying virtue is not that these people were the first to a new land or were born in a particular place. Ralph Waldo Emerson got close to the heart of the matter when he said, "Home is where your losses are," and this is painfully true for the Amerindians. Certainly I honor the depth of spiritual and emotional rootedness of peo-ple. But I am an ecologist, and my greatest respect is grounded in the ability of a person or a people to fit into a place, to adapt to the texture of the seasons, soils, and other life forms.

The word I seek is *indigenous*. According to my dic-tionary, *indigenous* is the quality of "having originated in and being produced, growing, living, or occurring natu-rally in a particular region or environment." It seems to me that one can "originate in" a place without having been born there. The origins of selfhood and relation-ships are not necessarily a function of one's birthplace. I yearn to grow so that I come to occur naturally in a place, to feel at home on the grasslands.

To have a home is to have special knowledge of a place that arises from first-hand experience. I began to call my house a home when it became part of my life through shared stories. Anyone could draw the floor plan, but we knew in which room our daughter and son slept on their first nights of life with us, which window was shattered by the ladder I was using while stringing Christmas lights, and which spots are favored by the cats on wintry mornings and summery afternoons. The hallway is filled with the photographic chronology of family life, the kitchen counter is stained where I cut strawberries to top the morning cereal, and the bedroom carpet is tinted blue where our son spilled paint while building his first model airplane on his own. Only we know that when the living room carpet is next peeled back and replaced, someone will find that we painted our names on the plywood floorboards to celebrate the completion of an interminable remodeling project.

If our house burned down, it could be rebuilt "as good as new," but the dings, scratches, and stains—the evidence of a family's memories—would be lost. It takes time to discover which corner of the house is the best sunny spot to read on a winter day (the cats providing key clues), to learn the complex lift-and-shove motion needed to open the screen door to the deck while keeping it on track, and to know when the hesitant draining in the kids' bathroom should prompt a preventive plungering of the toilet to avoid disaster.

For homes with a bit of land, a family soon learns which parts of the garden produce most reliably (plant spinach and radishes along the north side of the fence where the soil is cooler so they don't bolt in July, and plant carrots and beets near the kid's sandbox where the soil is well-drained and crumbly), where the lawn dries out first (near the blue spruce in the front yard), and where to build a good sled run from the back fence over the retaining wall and into the yard. Ethan knows just how to shoot a basketball from the corner of the driveway, arching the shot over the branch of the Russian olive and into the hoop. Erin knows where Snowball—the dwarf hamster that captured her heart and taught her about loving and dying—is buried. Just as our sphere of moral concern begins with our family and grows to encompass an ever-widening scope of fellow humans and creatures, so our sense of place starts at our hearth, expands into our yards and neighborhoods, and then reaches into our favorite picnic spots, fishing holes, and hiking trails.

With time, devotion, and attention I have learned what a wind from the east means for the coming weather, I can anticipate the first blooms of spring, and sometimes I know which bird is in a tree without seeing the songster. There are, I would respectfully suggest, European (and Asian and African) Americans who are truly indigenous. I accord these people the deep respect that is so often reserved for "native" Americans. Are not Edward Abbey and John Muir indigenous to their adopted homelands?

These icons of the West are not, however, indigenous to my corner of Wyoming. And so I find myself celebrating people like Larry Munn, a soil scientist in my department at the University of Wyoming who lives on a small ranch outside of town. He knows the geological story of the Laramie Valley, its fossil beds and glacial relics, its hollows and outcroppings, its grasses and shrubs, its rodents and ungulates, its thunderstorms and blizzards, its people and politics, and even its grasshoppers. He knows much more than I do. The first people to this valley are gone, and we must not forget how this happened. But the greater tragedy would be to fail to look forward, to wallow in guilt and shame for the past without cultivating a sense of Place among those who are here now.

The grasshoppers and first Americans colonized the land as the ice sheets receded about ten thousand years ago. Together they sculpted—and were sculpted by—

the landscape. Grasshoppers co-evolved with the grasses, herbs, and shrubs. Some specialized on particular plants by overcoming toxins that killed other herbivores. A few discovered ways of surviving the brutal winters so they could feast on the earliest spring growth before others even hatched. A handful of species adapted to life at timberline, taking two or more years to reach maturity in alpine meadows. Yet others became ever more elongated until they were nearly as thin as the grass stems and invisible to hungry birds. One species evolved into a locust, with the capacity to form migratory swarms that could eclipse the sun in great sweeps across the continent. And, almost certainly, some of the early species failed to match their biology to the land and so disappeared without a trace.

Surely, the first humans also struggled to find and create their relationship with the North American prairie. Although some of the early people over-exploited the large mammals that soon disappeared, others learned to use fire to create vast tracts of grasslands to nourish the bison. Some discovered that Mesoamerican plants could be cultivated and turkeys domesticated. And still others hunted and gathered, matching their movements and needs to the rhythms of the land. And so with time, these groups of humans either became in-digenous or they failed, leaving ghostly traces of their mistakes on canyon walls and cave floors.

We have much to learn from these indigenous people and creatures, but their world is no longer ours. We must discover for ourselves ways of living in a land with fences, roads, and power lines. It is easy to mock the neophyte who builds his house on top of a hill with north-facing windows devoid of winter sunlight and west-facing doorways opening into the prevailing winds. In my first year in Laramie, I planted peas on a false-spring weekend in April only to have the snows return and the seeds rot in the slush-soaked soil that didn't warm until early June. But my children know where to build a house and when to plant a garden.

Two hundred years after they arrived, had the first Americans discovered the limits of the herds, had they sorted out all of the edible and poisonous plants, had they mastered the materials of the land to perfect their shelters? The quick-and-sure costs of mistakes meant that the first people on this land had to become indige-nous very rapidly. We, on the other hand, have the lux-ury of imposing unsustainable technologies to buy time. But as reservoirs fill with silt, aquifers grow dry, soils erode, prairies are paved, and forests are cleared, we are coming to realize the limits of the land. They had wooly mammoths, we have fossil fuels—and both vanish in a geological moment. Ultimately, the culture arising from the second wave of immigrants has the same two choices that confronted the cultures that arose from the first wave. We can become indigenous or extinct. If we are not mindful in our pursuit of the former, our arrogance will not save us from the latter.

Xenophobia

I have been a stranger in a strange land.
—Exodus, 2:22

I TAKE PRIDE in having devoted my scientific life to the study of the Acrididae—the grasshoppers—one of the few insect families comprised entirely of native species in North America. These insects are ancient denizens of the grasslands—and the people of this landscape place particular value on "the way things have always been." Kathleen Norris, author of *Dakota: A Spiritual Geography*, wrote, "Wariness about change is a kind of prairie wisdom." In a modern culture that worships novelty, the dwellers of the North American steppe—those grasslands that are too cold, dry, and harsh to plow—are heretics.

The Protestant ideal of control and the ethic of work blended to form the founding principle of private property. The seventeenth-century moral philosopher John Locke argued that a claim of ownership is valid when a person mixes human labor with the land and thereby improves its value. This principle served as the basis of the Jeffersonian ideal of the yeoman farmer, who turned the soil and thereby transformed unruly grass into a well-ordered crop. Tilling the land and extracting a harvest were perceived as the most virtuous of all human endeavors. But we have discovered that there are limits to plowing the earth.

The life of the rancher unfolds on the rangeland, a community that ecologists refer to as a "polyculture of perennials," a robust mixture of native plants that hold the soil throughout the year. This contrasts with the predominant practice in American agriculture, growing a single annual crop that is uniformly susceptible to pests and that dies off during the winter, leaving the bare soil susceptible to erosion. This conceptually simple and ecologically profound difference between unbroken and broken grasslands helps to explain the nature of sustainability and the origin of the plainsman's wariness.

The farmer, by definition, changes the land and takes control of natural processes. The goal is to alter the earth to make it meet human needs. Left to its own, the land rarely produces abundant food for human consumption. Hunting and gathering can sustain small, mobile bands of people, but our civilization would collapse without the ability to convert wildlands into farmlands. Farming can be a noble venture when the farmer cultivates not only crops but also an understanding of what the land can sustain. But no matter the depth of awareness, farming necessitates an explicit imposition of our will on the world, the introduction of novelty. God-like, the farmer creates a garden. The rancher, however, conserves Creation.

In contrast to the farmer, the rancher succeeds to the extent that his or her work is unnoticed. By Locke's standard, the rancher would have no claim to ownership, because human labor has not "improved" the land. The well-managed ranch harvests the natural yield, taking only what is in abundance. Other than a few creaking windmills to fill stock tanks and some dusty two-track roads bordered by three-strand fences to confine the wandering cattle within pastures measured in terms of square miles, a good ranch is invisible. If I can stand atop a knoll, look to the horizon, and see no evidence that the grassland is changed from its natural state, I know that profound wisdom and unconventional work infuse the land. If the land is changed—by degradation of the grass cover, erosion of the soil, invasion of weeds, or loss of wildlife—the rancher has failed.

On the steppe, the measure of success is the lack of change. In a world addicted to progress, whatever its form, on the grasslands preservation is an ecological virtue and "staying put" is a social value. If our relationship to the land underlies our view of the world, then perhaps this explains why Wyoming is ranked as the most conservative state in the country. Wyomingites do not embrace change and progress—in grasslands or politics. Conserving the inmost qualities of a place is a virtue. But Henry David Thoreau reminds us that "we are double-edged blades, and every time we whet our virtue the return stroke straps our vice."

Nobody wants to be perceived as a stranger, outsider, barbarian, outcast, intruder, squatter, or interloper. But fear and loathing of foreigners have resurged with the arrival of terrorism on our shores. Despite desperate appeals for tolerance, this is not a good time to be an Arab or a Moslem in the United States. And I'll confess to an irrational surge of anxiety (followed by a flush of shame) when I'm boarding an airplane with fellow passengers who appear to be of Middle Eastern descent. But then,

Americans have always had a bit of ambivalence, if not antipathy, towards newcomers.

No matter what the Statue of Liberty proclaims about giving us your tired, poor, and huddled masses, the starving Irish were hardly welcomed in the 1840s and Chinese immigrants were banned in 1882. Today in the United States, we refer to "illegal immigrants" (a term that raises the odd matter of how a person, rather than an act, can be illegal) as aliens, as if they arrived from another planet to invade our safe and secure society. Even universities, the social bastions of free thinking, question whether there are "too many" foreign students.

There is intellectual relief but no moral solace in recognizing that we aren't unique in our bigotry. Consider that Australia excluded immigrants from Asia and Africa until 1965. For that matter, Europeans still struggle with accepting immigrants from these continents. And the French government has banned hajibs, yarmulkes, and crosses worn in public schools. Paul Flesher, a religious scholar, has suggested that this controversial policy derives from France's historical enmity between Church and State and the desire to protect French cultural integrity (religious differences are viewed as a risk to national loyalty).

Contemporary U.S. history textbooks offer a confused version of what it means to be a stranger, making it retroactively villainous to be a colonist but heroic to be an immigrant. As a grandson of immigrants and a social liberal in a very white and conservative state, I'll admit to my ambivalence. I'm here through a series of historical accidents, a regrettable but irreversible chain of events for the native people. On the other hand, now that I'm here and there's only so much room, we don't have to repeat the mistake.

Animal behaviorists, social psychologists, and anthropologists contend that latent xenophobia—the fear of new things, ideas, or people—is deeply engrained in my genetic predispositions. Like many other creatures, humans naturally avoid, even attack, unfamiliar beings. This appears to be an adaptive means of securing viable mates, protecting valuable territory, and avoiding dangerous predators. The logic is simple—the more someone looks like me, the more likely it is that he or she is related to me and thus the greater the chance that helping him or her will benefit my own genetic line. But it seems that modern xenophobia, although perhaps ancient in its origins, is more complex than the evolutionary story reveals.

My dislike for novelty is motivated by the blistering pace of change in the world, a turnover of knowledge, thoughts, ideas, inventions, and creations that leaves me dizzy and disoriented. Wall Street works hard to sell the idea that "new is good," but I'm wary about change. I've begun to feel like each day risks leaving me as a foreigner in a new land of technology, terminology, and taste. My sense of Place, an environment in which I feel grounded, is constantly eroded. As globalization homogenizes the world, I risk becoming vaguely familiar with everywhere but intimate with nowhere. The McDonalds on the Parisian street corner might be momentarily comforting, but then it becomes offensive. If Paris isn't foreign and exciting, then home isn't familiar and soothing. In an odd way, I want to feel like a stranger in other lands, but I'm uncomfortable with unfamiliar people in "my" downtown coffee shop—and with new species on my grasslands.

In the 1990s, I began a fight to keep the U.S. Department of Agriculture from introducing foreign fungal diseases and parasitic wasps to western rangeland as part of a government effort to suppress native species of grasshoppers. The conflict initially appeared to be a matter of science, with battles fought over the likelihood of these exotic organisms establishing themselves, the potential harm to ecological processes, and the possible impacts to plants, birds, and other creatures that depend on grasshoppers. The federal scientists were nonchalant about the exotic wasp or fungus displacing the native species, whose only value was in their advancement of human industry. The government auditors of ecology had deemed these native creatures to be "inefficient" workers in the rangeland factory—if they couldn't keep the grasshoppers in check, why then we'd hire some scab labor who'd do the job right.

As the war of words dragged on, the conflict became increasingly focused on values. Frustrated by my allusions to the transcendent value of the grasslands and its creatures, the USDA scientists argued that the purpose of the land was to serve human economies: "We are not particularly alarmed over the probabilities associated with such 'worst-case scenarios' as [the] major restructuring of plant communities [or the] annihilation or disruption of food chains or nutrient cycles in which grasshoppers are major participants." Soon, the disagreement was distilled to a fundamental difference regarding our relationship to the land. For my part, I finally admitted that the essential basis for my concerns was that the introduction of exotic species on a regional scale assaulted my sense of Place. The insect fauna of Wyoming grasslands had become more than an object of study—it had taken root in my sense of well-being. I found a potent ally in Eric Zencey, who maintained that scientists should,

> . . . acquire a kind of dual citizenship—in the world of ideas and scholarship [as well as] in the very real world of watersheds and growing seasons and migratory pathways and food chains and dependency webs. What is needed is a class of cosmopolitan educators willing to live where they work and work where they live, a class of educators willing to take root, willing to cultivate a sense of place.

Eventually, the USDA backed down from its plans to release parasitic wasps from Australia, and the initial releases of the exotic fungi were stopped. But spiritual notions of people and places were noncombatants in the war. My winning argument had to do with the likelihood that grasshopper species playing major roles in controlling populations of poisonous plants would be inadvertently suppressed, thereby releasing the weeds and causing widespread harm to livestock grazing on the rangelands. Without the sword of economics and the shield of industry, the aliens would have landed.

We are right to simultaneously cherish constancy and celebrate change. But, alas, ethics are traditionally grounded in reason, and paradox stands in defiance of logic. So perhaps it is time for our treasured standard of ethics to change. After all, the great German philosopher and intellectual architect of the Romantic movement, Friedrich Von Schelegel, maintained that "morality without a sense of paradox is mean." If it is true that the opposite of every great truth is another great truth, how can I sort out my love of the familiar from my fear of the strange? I've come to understand that despite our greatest struggles, authentic paradox cannot be resolved. The only escape comes in tolerating, then accepting, and finally embracing the glorious incongruity.

As for xenophobia, I simply do not know enough about the nature of the place that I hold dear nor about the qualities of new ideas, people, technologies, and creatures to justify my anxieties. I must confess that my fear of the strange is rooted in my ignorance. But is such uncertainty simply a recipe for moral paralysis? Not necessarily. After all, it's not the case that I don't know *anything*, rather it's a matter of realizing that I don't know *everything*. My course on "Great Books of the Life Sciences" is a discussion-based venture, and the first-day handout includes a set of "Principles of Participation," which includes the precept that, "I don't know everything and neither do you .... However, admitting the possibility that one's ideas are in error is entirely different than crawling within the shell of uncertainty." There is a critical difference between not knowing and not thinking.

So how should we respond to the strange, the foreign, the unfamiliar? This is surely one of the greatest challenges of the modern world, and there is no simple solution. We might begin by understanding the nature of our response to emerging ecological and social challenges. Retreat is often a tempting response. But the philosopher Ken Wilber gently and persuasively warns us that we cannot go backwards into a time before individuals were separate from forests, rivers, and prairies and liberated from the tribe, state, and church. As tempting as it might be when confronting new ways of being in the world, we cannot forget our selfhood—we cannot recover our lost innocence.

So, staying put is an enticing response. But digging in means becoming more deeply entrenched in what created the challenges we face. In ecological terms, voraciously consuming more manufactured goods will not remedy the anxiety of having become alienated from nature. And in a social context, jealously guarding the institution of marriage will not remedy the anxious feeling that we have become isolated from our gay and lesbian neighbors. To be differentiated from the natural world and from one another does not mean that we must become disassociated from vital relationships.

And so, moving forward is inevitable. We must discover or invent ways of responding to the ever-unfolding world so as to both honor our individuality and realize new forms of relationality. Wilber calls upon us to make whole beings from the imaginative integration of the familiar "self" and the strange "other." In a glorious paradox, the full realization of the self becomes possible through recognizing our utter dependence upon others. But to create authentic, transpersonal relationships, based on inter-being, is not a task at which we are well practiced.

I'm not a sociologist, so I don't know much about how we ought to go about re-conceiving human relations. But to be honest, many of our social "problems" with the unfamiliar and strange seem awfully simple, even borderline absurd. I just can't see the grave risks posed when a guy kisses another guy, a woman plays golf with men, or a girl wears a hajib to school. However, working out our ecological relations seems less obvious to me.

I understand the angst caused by exotic creatures on the prairie, snowmobiles in Yellowstone National Park, and wind farms on grassy knolls. The tension between constancy and change has, for me, metamorphosed into a sense of humility. And so, I can tentatively offer my own guidelines about how we might move forward in terms of human-nature relations. First, act slowly. Most changes are not made to avert an imminent crisis, and speed (like novelty) is not always a virtue. Second, move gently. We are much less likely to harm a person or place if we step lightly. Third, watch carefully. It is easier to reverse errors and alter directions if we catch a mistake early.

This isn't ethical rocket science but it's a start—after all, the Chinese stuffed bamboo tubes with gunpowder twenty-three hundred years before rockets carried humans to the moon. And the grasses offer their own lessons in humble starts and abiding patience: Fifty million years elapsed between the appearance of the first grasses and the terrestrial dominance of the grasslands.

Steppe Into the World

Our path leads through the steppe, through endless yearning,
Through your yearning, O Russia!
And I do not even fear the darkness
Of night beyond the border.
—Alexandr Blok

GRASS UNITES HUMANKIND. In the most fundamental sense, the staple foods of the world are based on
grasses. Humans may be divided by politics, but we're
united at the dinner table. The annual global harvest of
just four grasses—sugarcane, corn, rice, and wheat—is
greater than the total production of all 128 other food
crops grown on earth. These four grasses are harvested
from two million square miles of the earth's surface.
That's like planting a field extending from Canada to
Mexico and from the Mississippi to the Pacific. Although we've converted much of the grassland biome
into the breadbasket of humanity, nearly a quarter of the
land is still blanketed by native grasses in places that are

too dry and cold to plow—like most of Wyoming and Kazakhstan.

The grasslands evoke a paradoxical sense of austere abundance. The tall-grass prairies and other grasslands with rich soils have all virtually disappeared under the plow. So, what remains of these lands is too poor to support farming. Like the barrios of Rio de Janeiro or the slums of Calcutta, these ecological ghettos stretch far beyond the wealthy high rises of corn and sugar cane. The short- and mixed-grass prairies of the Great Plains still sweep eastward from the rocky spine of North America. The Pampas of Argentina evoke romance and high adventure, with even Charles Darwin falling under their spell during his voyage of discovery. Grasslands bristle along the edge of Australia's Outback like the continent's vast, day-old beard. It may be dwindling under the crush of human pressure, but Africa's savannah and the fabled Serengeti still host the most wondrous creatures to grace dry land: wildebeasts, zebras, giraffes, and lions. The rare, chalk grasslands of the British Isles are one of the few native ecosystems surviving in Europe. But nowhere captures the impoverished riches of the grasslands as do the steppes of Asia.

I count among my most valued days the time that I've spent on these lands. They lay like a frigid and voluptuous goddess—indifferent to our feeble courting, but ever-tempting in their beauty. I've witnessed the grandeur of the Mongolian plain, breathed the thin air of the Tibetan plateau, wandered the immensity of Siberia's steppe, surveyed the rolling hills of the Uzbek grasslands, and probed the boundless interior of Kazakhstan.

Like the grasses' ebb and flow with the abundant rains and searing droughts that cycle across the years, the people of the Asian steppe have periodically flourished and declined. Genghis Khan united the Mongolian tribes and swept across the grasslands with the most disciplined and brutal warriors the world had ever seen. In a matter of fifty years, the empire of the Khans stretched from Peking to Vienna, covering an area equal to seven-million square miles and encompassing one-fifth of the inhabited world. But the Mongols, great at conquest, were not much for administration.

In the latter half of the fourteenth century, an Uzbek prince, Timur-i-Leng, drove the Mongols from Central Asia and protected Europe from the Turks. The Europeans were so delighted that a statue was placed in Paris to honor their liberator—a chapter in history that, along with the statue, has been lost from Western culture. Timur's empire stretched from Russia to Persia and from present-day Turkey to India (Uzbek architects were the creative genius behind the Taj Mahal). Despite having eighteen wives, Timur had only four sons—it seems that being a ruler left little time for being a lover. His lands were divided among his sons, who proved less adept at ruling. In time, the Uzbek empire withered and dissolved, leaving a proud but fragmented collection of tribes.

There is a good reason why Timur nearly disappeared from Central Asian history—the next conqueror of the region labeled the Uzbek ruler a "criminal" and wiped clean the legend. In the brutal reign of Joseph Stalin, there was no allowance for cultural or ethnic pride. The Soviet Union reunited the people of Central Asia, and by some estimates the Soviets brought the region into the modern world. After the breakup of the USSR, the "stans" (Kazakhstan, Kyrgyzstan, Tajikistan, Turkmenistan, and Uzbekistan) undertook a redefinition of their stories, history being rewritten by the victors. Now just fourteen years into independence, these people are engaged in an epic tug-of-war trying simultaneously to assert their cultural autonomies while forging new political alliances. Although a new charismatic ruler seems unlikely to emerge as a catalyst for regional unity, another native inhabitant of these lands already appears to be filling this role to an extraordinary extent.

The four locust species of Central Asia have utter contempt for national boundaries, moving whimsically across borders to feed on grasslands and crops without regard to political claims. Tons of vegetation are moved from one country to another in the guts of locust swarms—perhaps the only import-export that avoids the scrutiny of the corrupt customs agents.

The most spectacular unification of nations via locusts comes rarely to this part of the world, but when it does there is no creature so completely overwhelming in power and scale. Outbreaks of the Desert locust can encompass all or part of sixty-two nations, comprising nearly a quarter of the earth's surface. The last such event to sweep across Central Asia was in 1962, although this invasion was a mere shadow of the plague that developed in 1929. Africa and the Middle East saw severe outbreaks of this species, and the human suffering was so extensive that the United Nations' Food and Agriculture Organization developed a program to battle Desert locusts in the 1960s.

Today, the fledgling nations of Central Asia focus their attention on less fantastic but more frequent incursions by other locust species.

An oddly named locust has recently forged links between Uzbekistan, Kazakhstan, and Russia, with each country quite certain that the swarms originate in its neighbor's lands. This insectan emissary is the Italian locust, an egregiously misnamed creature with but a passing connection to Italy via a specimen from southern Europe that served as the basis for the scientific name of the species some two centuries ago. Although the source of Italian locust outbreaks is a matter of some contention, everyone acknowledges the origin of Asia's most mobile (and appropriately named) locust species.

Swarms of the Migratory locust can travel up to fifteen hundred miles, from the Black Sea to the British Isles. If these cigar-sized creatures were scaled-up to human size, this journey would be equal to circumnavigating the earth in less than two months. The sources of these swarms are the reed beds along the shores of lakes and river deltas in Kazakhstan, Russia, and Uzbekistan. These are, in effect, the tallest grasses in the world, reaching heights of thirty feet and providing immense quantities of food for the locust's journeys.

Despite the Migratory locust's ability to link distant lands, the title of "insect ambassador of Central Asia" belongs to the Moroccan locust. This creature's outbreaks unite the farmers of Tajikistan with those of Kyrgyzstan as well as those of Afghanistan and Uzbekistan, with troublesome swarms occasionally emerging from Turkmenistan. This insect—like the Italian locust—is rather badly named. Morocco is the extreme western limit of its range. The locust's favored homeland is the rolling foothills of Central Asia, which is where I first met this remarkable creature.

Even before I left for a two-week trip to Central Asia in late March of 2003, I knew that Americans were not the most popular tourists in the world. With the war raging in Iraq, it was clear that we were at odds with most of the world's nations, and I'd heard of rather cold, if not nasty, receptions from colleagues traveling in Canada and Mexico. If our neighbors were that upset, then the Islamic countries of Central Asia would surely be even more explicit in their disapproval. I assured my family that I'd be safe, based on several thin lines of evidence. At least before I left, our State Department had not issued any warnings about travel to the region. I'd be traveling with Alex Latchininsky, my Russian co-worker who was familiar with this region from years of work in the area during Soviet times, and we'd be hosted by amiable colleagues in Kazakhstan and Uzbekistan. Moreover, the Food and Agriculture Organization of the United Nations was confidently sticking with their plan to meet in Termez. I was the only American citizen attending their locust management workshop, but presumably it would be very bad form to have an outside expert put in harm's way. Being an inveterate—but hopefully not terminal—idealist, I felt a strong pull to engage the people of the Islamic world during these difficult times.

In my mind, now was precisely the time for Americans who valued world peace and the integrity of the international community to travel abroad. Trusting the government and the media to represent me in these tense days seemed the worst of all ways to have a voice in the world. Although I was traveling under the auspices of science, I had no doubt that politics would enter into discussions between formal events. I wanted to explain for myself that many Americans were deeply disappointed in our government, that we respected other cultures, and that we valued nonviolent resolutions of conflict. The problem would be how to introduce these notions gracefully and diplomatically in the course of meetings in Almaty, Kazakhstan, and Termez, Uzbekistan.

Having worked extensively in France, Kazakhstan, Russia, Uzbekistan, and the United States, Alex was a consummate diplomat and profoundly sensitive to cultural nuances. In the 1980s, he spent months studying locusts in Central Asia and developing pest-management methods with local agencies and rural districts. He knew the people and their sensitivities. Under his tutelage, my plan was to studiously avoid initiating direct references to politics and to rehearse tactful replies to questions. But the most viable strategy was to prepare veiled allusions to politics for use in the private and public occasions, the American tendency for blunt and direct discourse being seen as tactless and offensive. The footings for the cross-cultural bridges that I prepared were based on a heartfelt commonality between our distant homes—the grasslands.

Our meeting in Almaty was really more of a celebration. Alex had edited a remarkable book entitled, *Guide to Locusts and Grasshoppers of Kazakhstan, Central Asia, and Adjacent Territories*, to which I'd contributed a chapter on pest management. His was the first book on this subject in fifty years, and it was clear that the people of the region were hungry, even famished, for reliable information on these insects. They were especially excited because the book was written in Russian, and we'd managed to provide two-thousand copies free to the relevant countries. So, the National Agricultural Library of Kazakhstan pulled out all the stops in organizing a book launch, complete with fresh flowers, a spectacular spread of food, plenty of vodka, traditional music and dancing, speeches, and television crews. In these last two contexts, my Americanism would be obvious through formal introductions and my lack of language skills. If there was no hiding that I was from a country at political odds with Kazakhstan, then the challenge was to earnestly convey that our people and lands had much in common.

The dignitaries were gathered around a thirty-foot conference table in a large hall, with an impressive crowd of onlookers packed into the far end of the room. Speakers from the government, scientific institutions, agricultural agencies, and foreign consulates all lauded the book. During my presentation, I had the odd advantage of requiring sequential translation. Delivering my ideas in discrete bursts allowed me to carefully watch and gauge the audience's response to my comments as they were interpreted. I began by thanking the organizers of the event, the sponsors of the project, and my co-authors. Then I thanked the grasshoppers and locusts. A wave of curious looks and furrowed eyebrows indicated that my unusual gratitude had been correctly translated. "Please allow me to explain," I continued:

> In a world so full of tension, unrest, and misunderstanding, the grasshoppers and locusts have provided a desperately needed element. These insects have served as our "common enemy." They provide a focus that has drawn people together from Kazakhstan, Uzbekistan, Russia, and the United States. Through the grasshoppers and locusts, we have found the means for genuine collaboration and authentic friendship among people.

At this point, there were some affirming nods. Bolstered by a sense that my translator was doing a fine job of getting my ideas across and that I'd hit a resonant chord with the assembly, I ventured on:

> To be accurate, the insects are not really our enemy. Rather, their damage is what we oppose.

And to be yet more accurate, what we battle against is human suffering. Our common enemies are not grasshoppers and locusts but hunger, poverty, and fear. And opposing these—rather than one another—is the true cause of science and humanity.

Returning to this area of the world, I am reminded how much we have in common. To begin, we share the open dialogue and mutual respect of scientists, a common desire to learn about the world, and a yearning to discover solutions to our common problems. Next, I would note that my home tucked between mountain ranges on the grasslands of Wyoming shares with your land many qualities. The prairies of Wyoming and the steppes of Kazakhstan have cold, clean air and warm, proud people. We both have glorious grasslands that stretch to the horizon, spectacular snow-covered mountains, and, of course, voracious grasshoppers.

Now, watching the people as they listened to my own words in Russian—a very strange experience indeed—I saw that they understood. Linking of people through the land and locusts made sense to them. Like most people in the world, they wanted to know that we had something in common. Maybe grasslands and grasshoppers aren't the typical tools of diplomacy, but I like to think that Wyoming and Kazakhstan aren't typical places.

I was interviewed by the anchor for the national news program, a very bright woman with coal-black hair and dazzling eyes, who wasn't easily satisfied with canned answers to her questions. She wanted to know why an American had been interested in raising funds for, and working on, a book about Kazakhstan. I first suggested that scientific inquiry draws people to distant lands, but she dismissed this easy appeal to intellectual curiosity and repeated the question. Next, I offered that scientists are concerned about the well-being of people around the world, but she was clearly unconvinced by altruistic motives. Again her interpreter pressed for an answer, emphasizing, "But why were you so interested?" I explained that the steppes of Wyoming and Kazakhstan were both beautiful and vibrant grasslands with much in common, so that whatever scientists learned in either country about grasshoppers or locusts could be valuable for the other. Finally, she smiled and nodded. In her search for my motive, academic interest was hardly persuasive and altruism was highly suspect, but having lands and locusts in common made sense.

The State Department warning came to me at precisely the wrong time and place. On the fourth of April, 2003, Americans were warned to defer travel to Uzbekistan and, in particular, to avoid places frequented by other foreigners in cities near the border zone with Afghanistan. All of this might have been useful information, except that I learned of the possible terrorist attacks on the ninth of April, while at the UN-sponsored workshop in Termez. This twenty-five-hundred-year-old city sits on the northern bank of the Amu Darya river. On the southern bank is Afghanistan. I received the travel advisory while at an internet café—a place where one might expect Americans and other foreigners to congregate. However, if terrorists had targeted every customer of internet cafés in Termez, exactly three people would have been at risk. That is the total number of public computer terminals in this city of sixty-two thousand residents.

The meeting was a great success—at least people from the six Central Asian nations were able to civilly discuss the sources of locust problems and plausible solutions. The only relevant country missing from the event was Russia, who was not invited to the workshop because they are not currently members of the Food and Agriculture Organization. There were wry smiles when it was noted that locusts are more global in their ecology than the United Nations is in its politics. Despite the intriguing nature of the structured discussions, after a couple days of having translations whispered in my ear in a stuffy meeting room, I was delighted to head into the hills to observe Moroccan locusts along with human efforts to suppress their infestations. A two-hour drive from Termez took us into the grasslands a few miles from the Tajikistan border. The temperature had dropped from the mid-nineties to the eighties. The intense emerald green of the rolling hills would be baked to a straw-yellow within a few weeks, but in spring the grasslands were sumptuous. With a light breeze whispering over the verdant knolls, I felt transported in time and space to a typical June day on the prairie back home.

The locusts were hatching in droves. On south-facing hillsides the bean-sized nymphs sprinkled the ground, and on exposed rocks they were packed into a solid blanket of bodies basking in the morning sun. Walking through a nursery of these tiny creatures stirred up a riot, as the nymphs peppered my legs from the knees down. Their wildly ricocheting bodies tumbled into the gaps around the tops of my shoes, and despite their desperate efforts to squirm free, my socks were soon plastered with squashed insects. In an area the size of a living room, there were twenty thousand infant locusts, each a nearly perfect, coffee-brown copy of the others.

Young men dressed in protective suits with gloves, masks, and goggles looked miserably hot as they sprayed a fog of insecticide from devices that were essentially re-engineered leaf blowers. The locusts boiled from under the men's feet. In an hour, the ground would be littered with tiny bodies. The outcome of this battle, like the war being fought a thousand miles to our west, was a foregone conclusion. And neither conflict—the battle with locusts nor the war with Iraq—was ever far from our minds or discussions. As much as the former clash promised to bring us together around a common enemy, the latter hostility threatened to divide us into opposing camps.

Returning from the grasslands to Termez, we stopped in the small town of Denau to visit the bazaar. As Alex and I were discussing locusts while standing in front of a vendor selling dried apricots, raisins, and almonds, we were approached by a woman in traditional dress. In sur-

prisingly good English, she asked if we were from En-
gland. I smiled and said, "No," not eager to volunteer my
nationality in a most unfamiliar setting. But she looked at
us with such expectancy that the silence was unbearable.

"I'm from the United States," I admitted, not wanting
to speak for Alex who has permanent residency but is
still a citizen of Russia.

Her face lit up. "America! That is wonderful. I teach
English at the school here. Now I tell . . . I told . . . no . . .
I will tell," she affirmed, proud of her grammatical reso-
lution, "my children that I meet someone from America.
It is so exciting for them to hear that."

As she was talking, an old man approached, his face
weathered to creased leather. Leaning on a gnarled cane
but looking remarkably animated for his apparent age,
he interrupted, "America?"

"Yes," I replied, thinking that surely he was going to
lambast me for my country's aggression. The teacher
quickly directed her conversation to Alex, respectfully
yielding to the old man and seemingly pleased to share
her newly discovered visitors.

"You know Los Angeles?" he asked me.

"Well, yes," I replied. His question seemed like a non
sequitur, but at least it wasn't a diatribe about imperial-

ism. Hoping that we were somehow connecting, I didn't want to explain that Los Angeles might have less in common with Laramie than Denau does.

"I know Los Angeles," he said proudly, "so we're friends."

"Have you been to Los Angeles?" I asked.

"Oh no," he replied gravely. "But I know of it." A grin spread across his face and his eyes twinkled. "So we're friends!"

Knowing the same place was all it took for this wise man to assert that he could be a friend. To share one thing with another person when you're ten thousand miles from home seems to be a fine condition for making friends. I might have chosen the grasslands, rather than Los Angeles, as a foundation for our newfound relationship, but I was delighted to acknowledge the City of Angels.

The people of Uzbekistan are quite adept at separating their outrage with U.S. policies from their reception of American citizens. I initially believed that this ability, often lacking in North America and Europe, arose from the political history of Central Asia. That is, these people were used to living under a non-representative government. For centuries, their leaders hadn't followed the will of the people, so why should they expect that I was in cahoots with the American president? But perhaps there was something deeper involved. Maybe ancient cultures of the grasslands understand that leaders flourish and die like the annual grasses and that politics blow with the wind. In the end, one must rely on sustaining good land and making good friends.

Song of the Loire

And I shall have some peace there, for peace comes dropping slow,
Dropping from the veils of the morning to where the cricket sings;
There midnight's all a glimmer, and noon a purple glow,
And evening full of the linnet's wings.
—William Butler Yeats

GRASSHOPPERS HAVE BROUGHT ME to the grasslands of the world: the steppes of Mongolia, the Tibetan
Plateau, the deserts of Kazakhstan, the Australian outback, the swards of Siberia, and the Brazilian cerrado.
To be more literal, but perhaps no more precise, the
study of grasshoppers has led me to these places. The
grasshoppers provide a reassuring presence, a connection to my homeland. Along with my familiar, insectan
escorts, there have been plenty of novel experiences. I
have dined on strips of sautéed pig's ear and barely clot-
ted blood-sausage, toasted my hosts with vodka made
from fermented mare's milk, weathered forty-mile-per-
hour winds in 120-degree heat, and cancelled a flight

into Asmara because the Ethiopians were bombing the airport. My only regret is that these adventures have been without my human loved ones.

But last year, grasshoppers guided me to a place where my family could join the adventure—France. Montpellier hosted the seventh International Meeting of the Orthopterists Society, a bonafide scientific association comprised of about three hundred people from nearly fifty nations—all of whom, incredible as it may seem, devote their professional lives to the study of grasshoppers, crickets, and katydids. The conference was fine, even spectacular in terms of the program and facilities, but I discovered things more important and less expected on the way to the event. Our amble from Paris to the Mediterranean took us through the heart of the French countryside. And for a romantic entomologist, the Loire Valley offered more than the best scientific presentations in the most exquisite of meeting halls.

France is, above all else, sensual. During a week of bicycling in the Loire Valley, we discovered that this magical place tastes as rich as the cuisine of the kings who dotted the landscape with their chateaux, and it smells like an earthy floral infusion. The valley feels as hard as the stone walls of the countryside and as soft as the tilled soil of the fields. A vista of rolling hills covered by a quilt of emerald green and golden brown under an azure sky is a feast for the eyes. But it was the sounds of this enchanting land—the soothing hum of life—that became indelibly linked with my memories of the fields, glades, and villages.

France is a great place to be an entomologist. I am used to people not taking me seriously—how can a man who never outgrew chasing grasshoppers be a threat? And it seems that France embraces the unconventional, the quirky, and the eccentric. After all, the country produced Jean Henri Fabre, a man who devoted his life to the meticulous study of the insects in the pebbly, untilled lands near the village of Sérignan in the early 1900s. Too poor to travel, he spent the last thirty-odd years of his life recording his painstaking observations, simple experiments, and remarkable insights within a couple hours' walk of his home. What emerged is a set of the most lyrical and gracious essays on the natural world that have ever been produced. So it was that a humble hamlet, not a celebrated city, produced this national treasure. For our part, we found Paris bustled with the vibrant sounds of people, and Blois murmured like the river flowing past the city's winding streets. But the

Loire Valley—nestling the serene village of Chitenay, where we found a cozy refuge on the second floor of the Auberge de Centre—was infused with natural romance, the love songs of insects.

Sunrise in the Loire Valley belongs to the birds. The insects and I wake more slowly. My idea of a vacation agrees with the dictionary definition: an interval of rest or relief. Not so for my family. By 7:30, Nan and the kids are ready for a basket of fresh croissants—an indulgence that we justify with our daily fifteen- to forty-mile bicycle rides. Pedaling along the country lanes immerses us in the landscape. Without the drone of traffic (it is possible to ride for half an hour without encountering a car), the peal of church bells in the villages and the hum of a tractor in the field are carried along with chirps and twitters on the whispering breeze. By mid-morning, the grasshoppers begin to climb to the swaying seed heads of meadow grasses and move onto the gravelly roadsides, as if in search of the strong, black coffee that stimulated my earlier activity. But it is not food or drink that they pursue. Rather the grasshoppers seek heat, basking in the warmth of the sun and tuning their fiddles for the day's concert. The first, tentative buzzing and strumming comes from the dew-sparkled grasses at ten thirty.

By noon, the grasshoppers are usually in full song. But when the day starts out cloudy and the sun doesn't break through until midday, the grasshoppers sleep in. Once the sun melts through the clouds and its rays streak the sky and brighten the fields, the songsters are frantic to make up for lost time. In the radiance following a light morning sprinkle, the rain-washed air seems to carry colors, fragrances, and sounds with crystal clarity. The midday chirps, hums, and rattles take on special exuberance.

There's one species of grasshopper that does a perfect imitation of the clicking free-wheel on a coasting bicycle. I overlook the presence of this remarkable mimic until I am bringing up the rear and find it odd—and mechanically impossible—that this machine-like ticking persists even while we are all pedaling. A day or so after my first suspicions of a mechanical mimic, I confirm the origin of this clicking during a water-and-baguette break. We are all dismounted when the little scamp (a tiny katydid with chocolate-brown stripes and absurdly overgrown hindlegs) launches into its version of "The Coasting Cycle Roundelay."

The other grasshoppers are equally evocative in their songs. Some meadows reverberate with the sounds of Lilliputian jack-hammers. Stopping for a picnic of cheese and fresh fruit, I feel compelled to search the grass for an elfin man scolding us with a clucking tongue for intruding on his meadow. With persistence, I discover that the meadow is not enchanted; rather, a grasshopper is responsible for the chiding "tch-tch-tch." After lunch, the grasshoppers maintain the fairytale ambience, their back-and-forth songs from the roadsides giving the impression that dozens of gnomes are hiding in the wildflowers, rubbing their fingers along variously sized combs, sending messages in some secret code. Other stretches of road greet us with the rattling of tiny maracas or the rather less fantastical clattering of stuck electrical relays.

To hear my favorite grasshopper of the Loire Valley, say *visit* as fast as you can three or four times in succession. When the vowel sounds compress to nothingness and the word is pure consonants, you have it. To imitate being there, take life as slowly as possible three or four days in a row. "You are a sentimentalist," my critics will contend, as if romance is a false path to understanding or truth is the exclusive purview of reason. Can spending long, pointless hours with loved ones be a rational experience? Could a serenade in an Impressionistic meadow or a rhapsody in the tranquil countryside be anything other than romantic?

In the afternoon, the Loire Valley becomes a symphony with distinct movements. There is the serenity of the forest glades that dot the landscape. As the road enters the stillness of the woods, a silence prevails. But not all silences are the same. The stillness of an empty house can be unnerving, but this quietness is profoundly soothing. Invariably our pace slows, as we try to absorb and store the coolness. The silence is broken only by the hum of our tires and erratic, metallic chirps from the overhanging canopy of branches—perhaps the call of a lonely katydid or a lustful tree-frog.

Emerging into the brilliant sunlight, the earned sweat of the fields replaces the complimentary dampness of the forest. With the heat comes the insistent "chk-chk" alongside the hayfields, the lazy "bzz . . . bzz . . .bzz" among the poppies, and the sporadic ticking arguments in the grainfields. The vineyards are the rests in the musical score. It seems that the grasshoppers don't find much to their liking among the grapes, which is one element of their lives that I simply can't understand.

Resting in the shade of a tree-lined avenue, we listen for the last of the summer's cicadas. The initially uncoordinated efforts of a few spirited individuals are reminiscent of a symphony's discordant warm-up. But it seems that an insectan conductor amidst the branches cannot stand the cacophony. And so, the individual fits and starts soon synchronize into a pulsing, throbbing song—an ebb and flow that washes over the sleepy, sun-drenched village.

Evening brings a softness to the French countryside. Back at our hotel, we luxuriate on the patio, savoring each course of dinner and listening to the insectan love songs in the garden. On these warm nights, their trills are a perfect accompaniment to the elegant clink of silver on china and the ripples of French conversation. It is as if the humans and the insects of France have reached a most graceful and refined linguistic compromise—the humans speak in vowel-suffused murmurs and the crickets chirp in consonant-spattered staccato. The tranquility is punctuated by the cheerful popping of a cork, announcing the arrival of an exquisite wine nurtured and bottled by one of the vintners through whose land we rode today.

I look at my son, who is trying to scoop the last molecule of strawberry sorbet from his bowl. My gaze drifts over to my daughter, who is trying to overhear a child's conversation at the next table to test her budding French. Then I watch my wife penning a postcard to friends back home. I close my eyes and I find myself making a sound that has become all too rare in life—a sigh of pure contentment. As the last glow of dusk starts to fade, we too begin to wane and head up to our snug room, serenaded by the crickets still in search of lovers.

When morning comes, stiff thighs and sore rears are once again set in motion, and I look forward to a day of being intrigued, incurrent, inspired, incarnate, incomputable—in love. Jean Henri Fabre captured the essence of France for romantic entomologists. In *Life of a Grasshopper*, he wrote,

> I see in the Grasshopper's fiddle, the Tree-frog's bagpipes and the cymbals of the Cacan (Cicada) but so many methods of expressing the joy of living, the universal joy which every animal species celebrates after its own kind.

Simple creatures manifesting a "joy of living"—can this be the interpretation of a scientist? Perhaps. After all, in explaining his theory of evolution, Charles Darwin proposed that "The vigorous, the healthy, and the happy survive and multiply." Fabre's writings leave no doubt

that he had a keen mind and the ability to deduce scientific insights from hours of patient, objective observations. But he was unwilling to limit himself to this single
way of knowing the world. Reason could take him only
so far. What of the elements of nature that stretched
beyond what logic could reveal? It is fitting that a French
naturalist would find that the romance of grasshoppers
was irreducible to the Laws of Science:

> What purpose is served by the Grasshopper's mu-
> sical instrument? I will not go so far as to refuse it
> a part in the pairing, or to deny it a persuasive
> murmur, sweet to her who hears it; it would be
> flying in the face of evidence. But this is not the
> principal function. Before anything else, the insect
> uses it to express its joy in living, to sing the de-
> lights of existence with a belly well filled and a
> back warmed by the sun, as witnessed by the big
> Decticus and the male Grasshopper, who, after the
> wedding, exhausted for good and all and taking no
> further interest in pairing, continue to strum mer-
> rily so long as their strength holds out.

And so as we head off for another ride, my daughter
and I strike up a silly ditty, a truly absurd sequence of

lyrics that she learned from a pair of storytelling minstrels one night, well past her bedtime, a year ago, in a musty barn converted to a student lounge, at the smallest college in the United States. This song serves no purpose—other than to express our joy of living.

Fabre would understand.

Epilogue

College students determined to convert their educational years into lucrative careers major in business and finance, generally avoid the eccentric world of grasshoppers and the austere ecology of grasslands. But when in the name of liberal education the University required all students to take a science course, the institution unwittingly created a curricular niche. And if entomologists have learned anything from insects, it is how to exploit an empty niche. We created a course called "The Biodiversity Crisis," which turned out to be a rip-roaring success. Our enrollment triumph (more than a hundred students) was almost surely because business majors saw the course as a way of avoiding the drudgery of General Biology. The goal was to get students thinking about how humans change, and are changed by, the natural world. I knew it would be a challenge to induce deep contemplation, but I hoped to at least convey the value of nature in the circumscribed terms of federal law.

The Endangered Species Act is daunting, but students soon comprehend habitat conservation plans and incidental take permits. However, at the core of the Act lies a precept so alien to their worldview that many are unable to internalize this basic principle. Despite judicial rulings that the Act places no limit on the worth of other life forms and the places they need to survive, students remain incredulous. They can imagine the justification for saving the home of the spotted owl—who isn't humbled in the presence of old-growth forest? But a tract of barren sandhills that are the last sanctuary of an unremarkable grasshopper species—especially when the land could be used for something sensible like housing people rather than harboring insects—is another matter altogether. When asked on an exam what value the law ascribes to a parcel of desolate grassland needed by the last remnants of a lowly species (such as a grasshopper), one-third of the students insist on an answer that converts the insects' home into dollars. And so, while my students readily grasp legal theory, refusing a million dollars for the last acre of a creature's habitat is, for many, inconceivable.

Some of my students have the potential to become truly gifted thinkers, and with the dedicated efforts of the University's faculty, these students can cultivate and refine their analytical skills. But therein lies the difficulty, for as the Zen teacher noted, "Reason can only work with the experience that is available to it." And it takes more than a semester, more than four years—perhaps more than a lifetime—to come to know a land and its creatures.

Acknowledgments

This, my second collection of essays, is a bit like a second date. I worried that maybe all of my most engaging thoughts, evocative allusions, and endearing tales were already spent. But a relationship develops with a genuine dialogue, and the enthusiastic response to my first book, *Grasshopper Dreaming: Reflections on Loving and Killing*, was sufficient to convince me that it was worth the risk of a second date. And so, I'd like to thank all of the people who read my first venture and provided the words—by voice, pen, and email—that encouraged me to continue my writing.

I want to gratefully acknowledge my institution—the Department of Renewable Resources, the College of

Agriculture, and the University of Wyoming—and those administrators who think that a scientist is justified in writing about important, heartfelt matters. In this regard, I also deeply appreciate my scientific and academic communities, especially: my staff who kept the real work of science going while I was writing, those students who showed enthusiasm for my efforts, and the faculty who expressed support for their unusual colleague.

And I offer my most profound gratitude to my family. Their love and understanding fill my life and create the safe place within which I can savor the act of writing. They are proud of my work, and that means a great deal more than I can possibly express.

I also give thanks to the people of the Unitarian Universalist Fellowship of Laramie for their warmth, encouragement, and validation of who I am and what I do. Being a good congregation, their affection is unconditional—but they do not abide mushy thinking or platitudinous emoting. They are a wonderful audience to have in mind while writing.

Finally, I must thank Mary Benard and the rest of the folks at Skinner House who worked hard to put my writing in your hands. Their understanding, insight, and collaboration were invaluable. A writer may produce gems, but their beauty depends on the cutting and polishing skills of a gifted editor.